SHAH MOHAMMED

The Disruptive Innovation Formula

Strategies to Create Disruptive Innovation in Your Business

Copyright © 2024 by Shah Mohammed

All rights reserved. No part of this publication may be reproduced, stored or transmitted in any form or by any means, electronic, mechanical, photocopying, recording, scanning, or otherwise without written permission from the publisher. It is illegal to copy this book, post it to a website, or distribute it by any other means without permission.

First edition

This book was professionally typeset on Reedsy.
Find out more at reedsy.com

Contents

Introduction — iv
1. Targeting Noncustomers — 1
2. Observing Extremes and Outliers — 11
3. Targeting Next-Generation Customers — 20
4. Anticipate Future Trends/Needs — 26
5. Democratizing Access — 32
6. Reimagining Customer Experience — 40
7. Simplifying Customer Journeys — 48
8. Hyper-Personalization — 56
9. Tracking Emerging Technologies — 63
10. Tracking Emerging Competitors — 72
11. Reimagining Business Models — 78
12. Convergence of Industries — 91
13. Circular Economy — 97
14. Shared Economy — 102
15. Gamification — 109
16. Reverse Innovation — 118
17. Breaking Functional Fixedness — 125
18. Kill Your Own Business — 131

About the Author — 137
Also by Shah Mohammed — 139

Introduction

In today's fast-paced, technology-driven business landscape, disruptive innovation has become a critical factor in determining a company's success or failure. Disruptive innovation refers to the creation of new products, services, or business models that fundamentally transform industries and reshape consumer expectations. It often starts with a simple idea or a niche market, but gradually gains momentum until it displaces established players and becomes the new industry standard.

From Netflix disrupting the entertainment industry to Airbnb revolutionizing travel accommodations, examples of disruptive innovation are all around us. These companies succeeded not by incrementally improving existing products or services, but by anticipating future trends, targeting underserved customers, and reimagining entire industries. They challenged conventional wisdom, embraced new technologies, and created value in ways that were previously unimaginable.

However, for every successful disruptor, there are countless established companies that failed to adapt to changing market conditions and customer needs. Blockbuster, Kodak, and BlackBerry are just a few examples of once-dominant firms that were overtaken by more innovative competitors. In an age of rapid technological advancement and shifting consumer preferences, no company is too big to fail or too established to be disrupted.

The purpose of this book is to provide a short guide to the strategies that companies can use to create disruptive innovations and stay ahead of the curve. Drawing on extensive research and real-world examples, we will explore a wide range of topics, from anticipating future trends and observing extreme users to reimagining business models and breaking functional fixedness.

Whether you are an entrepreneur looking to launch a groundbreaking startup or an established company seeking to reinvent yourself in the face of industry disruption, this book will provide you with the insights you need to succeed.

Throughout the book, we will emphasize the importance of a customer-centric approach to innovation. Disruptive innovation is not about technology for technology's sake, but about creating value for customers in new and meaningful ways. By deeply understanding customer needs, pain points, and aspirations, companies can identify untapped opportunities and create innovations that resonate with their target audience.

Ultimately, the goal of this book is to inspire and equip you to become a disruptive innovator in your own industry. Whether you are a seasoned executive or a young entrepreneur, the strategies and frameworks presented here will help you navigate the challenges and opportunities of the 21st-century business landscape. By embracing disruptive innovation, you can not only survive but thrive in an age of unprecedented change and uncertainty.

So, let's dive in and explore the exciting world of disruptive innovation together. The future belongs to those who dare to imagine it and create it.

* * *

1

Targeting Noncustomers

Disruptive innovation often stems from identifying and serving untapped or underserved markets. By focusing on noncustomers – those who are not currently consuming a product or service due to various barriers or constraints – companies can uncover new opportunities for growth and create disruptive offerings that challenge industry norms.

Noncustomers

The term "noncustomers" refers to potential customers who are not currently consuming a company's products or services due to various barriers, constraints, or unmet needs. These individuals or groups represent untapped market opportunities that are often overlooked by established players in an industry.

Noncustomers can be classified into three main categories:

1. **Underserved Noncustomers:** These are people whose needs are not adequately met by existing offerings in the market. They may find current products or services too complex, expensive, or inconvenient and thus choose not to consume them. Underserved noncustomers present an opportunity for companies to develop simpler, more affordable, or

more accessible solutions that address their specific needs.
2. **Overserved Noncustomers:** These are people who find current offerings in the market too sophisticated, feature-rich, or expensive for their needs. They may be paying for features or benefits they don't actually require and would prefer a more streamlined, basic, or cost-effective solution. Overserved noncustomers present an opportunity for companies to introduce simplified, lower-cost alternatives that better align with their preferences.
3. **Unserved Noncustomers:** These are people whose needs are not addressed by any existing offerings in the market. They may belong to customer segments that have been entirely ignored or overlooked by industry players. Unserved noncustomers present an opportunity for companies to create entirely new markets by developing innovative solutions that cater to their unique needs and constraints.

By targeting noncustomers, companies can tap into new sources of growth and disrupt established industries. This requires a deep understanding of the needs, preferences, and pain points of these untapped market segments, as well as a willingness to challenge conventional wisdom and develop innovative solutions that address their specific requirements.

Successful disruptive innovators often begin by targeting noncustomers, as these segments are typically less contested and more receptive to new, unconventional offerings. By gaining a foothold with noncustomers, these companies can build momentum, refine their solutions, and eventually expand into mainstream markets, displacing established players and transforming entire industries.

The Process

Identifying noncustomers, understanding their needs and constraints, and developing solutions for them is a critical process in creating disruptive innovation.

Step 1: Identifying Noncustomers

- **Analyze the Market:** Begin by thoroughly examining the existing market and identifying the customer segments that are currently being served by the industry players. Look for gaps or underserved areas in the market that could represent potential noncustomers.
- **Conduct Market Research:** Engage in extensive market research to gather data on consumer behavior, preferences, and pain points. Use surveys, focus groups, and interviews to gain insights into the reasons why certain individuals or groups are not consuming the products or services offered in the market.
- **Look Beyond the Obvious:** Don't limit your analysis to the immediate industry or market. Investigate adjacent industries, substitute products, and alternative solutions that may be meeting the needs of potential noncustomers in different ways.
- **Identify Barriers to Consumption:** Examine the various barriers that prevent potential customers from consuming the products or services in the market. These barriers could include price, accessibility, complexity, lack of awareness, or cultural factors.
- **Segment Noncustomers:** Categorize noncustomers into distinct segments based on their common characteristics, needs, and constraints. This segmentation will help you develop targeted solutions that address the specific requirements of each noncustomer group.

Step 2: Understanding Noncustomer Needs and Constraints

- **Empathize with Noncustomers:** Put yourself in the shoes of noncustomers and strive to understand their perspective. Use ethnographic research methods, such as observing noncustomers in their natural environment or conducting in-depth interviews, to gain a deeper understanding of their needs and challenges.
- **Identify Jobs-to-be-Done:** Focus on the underlying jobs or tasks that noncustomers are trying to accomplish, rather than just the products or

services they are using. Understanding the functional, emotional, and social dimensions of these jobs will provide valuable insights into their unmet needs.

- **Map Customer Journey:** Create a detailed map of the noncustomer's journey, from initial awareness to post-purchase experience. Identify the pain points, obstacles, and moments of frustration that noncustomers encounter along the way.
- **Analyze Constraints:** Examine the various constraints that noncustomers face, such as limited budget, time, expertise, or access to resources. Understanding these constraints will help you develop solutions that are feasible and attractive to noncustomers.
- **Seek Out Extreme Users:** Pay attention to extreme users or edge cases, as they often have the most pronounced unmet needs and can provide valuable insights into potential disruptive opportunities.

Step 3: Developing Solutions for Noncustomers

- **Ideate and Brainstorm:** Engage in creative brainstorming sessions to generate a wide range of potential solutions that address the identified needs and constraints of noncustomers. Encourage unconventional thinking and challenge existing assumptions.
- **Simplify and Streamline:** Look for ways to simplify, streamline, or repackage existing products or services to make them more accessible, affordable, or convenient for noncustomers. Remove unnecessary features or complexity that may be barriers to adoption.
- **Explore New Business Models:** Consider alternative business models that could better align with the needs and preferences of noncustomers. This could include subscription-based models, pay-per-use, or freemium offerings.
- **Leverage Technology:** Investigate how emerging technologies, such as artificial intelligence, mobile platforms, or cloud computing, could be leveraged to create innovative solutions that address the needs of noncustomers in new and disruptive ways.

- **Co-Create with Noncustomers:** Involve noncustomers in the solution development process through co-creation workshops, beta testing, or pilot programs. This collaborative approach ensures that the developed solutions resonate with the target noncustomer segments.
- **Iterate and Refine:** Continuously iterate and refine the developed solutions based on feedback from noncustomers. Embrace a lean and agile approach to product development, allowing for rapid prototyping, testing, and improvement cycles.
- **Validate and Scale:** Validate the effectiveness of the developed solutions through rigorous testing and market validation. Once proven successful, develop strategies to scale the solutions and capture a larger share of the noncustomer market.

By following this systematic approach to identifying noncustomers, understanding their needs and constraints, and developing targeted solutions, companies can unlock new opportunities for growth and disruptive innovation. It is important to remember that this process is iterative and requires continuous learning, adaptation, and refinement based on market feedback and changing customer preferences.

Nintendo Wii

Before the launch of the Nintendo Wii in 2006, the video game industry was primarily focused on catering to hardcore gamers. Sony's PlayStation and Microsoft's Xbox were the dominant players, offering high-end graphics, complex gameplay, and mature content. The target audience for these consoles was typically young males aged 18-35 who were dedicated gamers.

Identifying Noncustomers: Nintendo recognized that there was a significant untapped market of potential customers who were not being served by the existing gaming consoles. These noncustomers included:

1. **Casual Gamers:** People who enjoyed playing video games but were

intimidated by the complexity and learning curve of traditional gaming consoles.
2. **Older Adults:** The 35+ age group who had grown up with classic Nintendo games but had lost touch with gaming as they aged and found modern consoles too complex.
3. **Women:** Many women were not attracted to the violent, male-oriented content that dominated the gaming market.
4. **Families:** Parents who wanted to enjoy gaming with their children but found the content and complexity of existing consoles unsuitable for family play.

Understanding Noncustomer Needs and Constraints: Nintendo conducted extensive market research to understand the needs and constraints of these noncustomer segments. They found that noncustomers wanted:

1. **Simplicity:** A gaming console that was easy to set up, navigate, and play without requiring a steep learning curve.
2. **Accessibility:** Games that were approachable for people of all ages and skill levels, without the need for prior gaming experience.
3. **Social Interaction:** A gaming experience that encouraged social interaction and could be enjoyed with friends and family.
4. **Intuitive Controls:** A control system that was intuitive and mimicked real-life motions, rather than complex button combinations.
5. **Affordable Pricing:** A console that was affordable for families and casual gamers who were not willing to invest heavily in gaming hardware.

Developing Solutions for Noncustomers: Based on these insights, Nintendo developed the Wii console with features specifically designed to address the needs of noncustomers:

1. **Motion Control:** The Wii Remote introduced motion-based controls that allowed players to interact with games using natural, intuitive movements. This made the gaming experience more accessible and

engaging for noncustomers.

2. **Wii Sports:** Nintendo bundled the Wii console with Wii Sports, a collection of five sports-based games that showcased motion control capabilities. These games were easy to learn, fun to play, and appealed to a wide range of noncustomers.
3. **Inclusive Content:** Nintendo focused on developing games that were family-friendly, non-violent, and appealed to a broad audience. Titles like Wii Fit, Mario Kart Wii, and Super Mario Galaxy attracted noncustomers who had previously been excluded from gaming.
4. **Affordable Pricing:** Nintendo priced the Wii console significantly lower than its competitors, making it more accessible to price-sensitive noncustomers.
5. **Viral Marketing:** Nintendo's marketing campaigns showcased the social and interactive aspects of the Wii, featuring people of all ages and backgrounds enjoying the console together. This approach resonated with noncustomers and created a buzz around the Wii.

Impact and Results: The Nintendo Wii's focus on noncustomers was a resounding success, disrupting the gaming industry and expanding the market to new audiences. Some of the key results include:

1. **Market Expansion:** The Wii brought millions of new players into the gaming market, many of whom had never owned a gaming console before.
2. **Sales Success:** The Wii sold over 101 million units worldwide, surpassing the sales of both the PlayStation 3 and Xbox 360 during the same generation.
3. **Cultural Impact:** The Wii became a cultural phenomenon, with people of all ages and backgrounds engaging with the console. It was common to see families, seniors, and casual gamers playing the Wii together at home, in retirement homes, and even in rehabilitation centers.
4. **Industry Influence:** The success of the Wii prompted other gaming companies to reconsider their strategies and develop more inclusive,

motion-based gaming experiences.

Nintendo's approach to targeting noncustomers with the Wii is a prime example of how understanding and addressing the needs of untapped market segments can lead to disruptive innovation and significant business success. By challenging the status quo and creating a gaming experience that resonated with a broader audience, Nintendo expanded the gaming market and solidified its position as a leader in the industry.

Airbnb

Before the launch of Airbnb in 2008, the travel accommodation industry was dominated by traditional hotels and resorts. These establishments catered primarily to travelers who valued consistency, predictability, and a standardized experience. The cost of staying in hotels, especially in popular tourist destinations, was often quite high, making travel unaffordable for many people.

Identifying Noncustomers: Airbnb recognized that there was a significant untapped market of potential customers who were not being served by the traditional hotel industry. These noncustomers included:

1. **Budget-conscious travellers:** People who wanted to travel but could not afford the high costs of hotel accommodations.
2. **Experience-seekers:** Travelers who wanted a more authentic, immersive experience and the opportunity to live like a local in the destinations they visited.
3. **Guests seeking unique accommodations:** Those who were looking for unconventional lodging options, such as treehouses, boats, or historical properties, which hotels did not typically offer.
4. **Homeowners with extra space:** People who had unused rooms, apartments, or entire homes that could be rented out to travelers, providing a new source of income.

Understanding Noncustomer Needs and Constraints: Airbnb conducted extensive research to understand the needs and constraints of these noncustomer segments. They found that noncustomers wanted:

1. **Affordability:** Accommodations that were more affordable than traditional hotels, allowing them to stretch their travel budgets further.
2. **Authentic experiences:** The opportunity to stay in local neighborhoods, interact with hosts, and experience the destination like a local.
3. **Variety:** A wide range of unique accommodation options that catered to different preferences and budgets.
4. **Trust and safety:** A platform that provided a trusted, secure way to book accommodations and communicate with hosts.

Developing Solutions for Noncustomers: Based on these insights, Airbnb developed a platform that addressed the needs of noncustomers:

1. **Peer-to-peer platform:** Airbnb created a platform that connected travelers with local hosts who had extra space to rent out. This allowed for a wide variety of affordable accommodations in destinations around the world.
2. **User reviews and ratings:** Airbnb implemented a review system that allowed guests and hosts to rate each other, fostering trust and transparency within the platform.
3. **Unique accommodation options:** The platform encouraged hosts to list a wide range of unique properties, from apartments and houses to treehouses, boats, and castles. This variety appealed to experience-seeking noncustomers.
4. **Local experiences:** Airbnb expanded its offerings to include local experiences hosted by residents, allowing travelers to immerse themselves in the local culture and connect with the community.

Impact and Results: Airbnb's focus on noncustomers revolutionized the travel accommodation industry and led to significant growth and success for the company:

1. **Market disruption:** Airbnb disrupted the traditional hotel industry by providing a more affordable, diverse, and authentic alternative for travelers.
2. **Global expansion:** The platform rapidly expanded to thousands of cities worldwide, offering accommodations in over 220 countries and regions.
3. **Increased accessibility to travel:** By providing affordable accommodation options, Airbnb made travel more accessible to a broader range of people, including those who may have previously been priced out of the market.
4. **Economic empowerment:** Airbnb provided a new source of income for hosts, allowing them to monetize their extra space and benefit from the tourism industry.

By providing a platform that offered affordability, variety, and authentic experiences, Airbnb disrupted the travel accommodation industry and unlocked a new market of travelers who had previously been underserved.

In conclusion, targeting noncustomers is a powerful strategy for creating disruptive innovation. By identifying underserved or overlooked market segments, understanding their unique needs and constraints, and developing tailored solutions, companies can unlock new opportunities for growth and transform entire industries. While serving noncustomers comes with its own set of challenges and risks, the potential rewards – in terms of market share, customer loyalty, and long-term competitive advantage – make it a strategy worth pursuing for businesses seeking to drive disruptive change.

* * *

2

Observing Extremes and Outliers

When seeking to create disruptive innovation, it's essential to look beyond the mainstream and pay close attention to the fringes of your target market. By observing the extreme users and outliers within your industry, you can gain valuable insights into unmet needs, untapped opportunities, and potential areas for disruption. These individuals often have the most pronounced pain points and are more likely to embrace unconventional solutions that challenge the status quo.

Extremes and outliers refer to individuals or data points that lie far outside the norm or average in a given context. In the realm of innovation and product development, these terms are used to describe users or customers who have unique, unconventional, or highly specific needs, behaviors, or preferences that deviate significantly from the majority of the target market.

Extreme users are those who push the boundaries of how a product or service is typically used. They may have needs that are not adequately addressed by existing solutions, face unusual constraints, or employ the offering in unconventional ways. For example, in the context of a fitness tracking app, an extreme user might be a professional athlete who requires advanced features and highly detailed performance data.

Outliers, on the other hand, are users or data points that are significantly different from the rest of the population. They may have unique characteristics, behaviors, or preferences that set them apart from the mainstream. For instance, in the context of a music streaming service, an outlier might be a user who listens exclusively to a niche genre of music that is not well-represented in the platform's catalogue.

By studying these individuals, companies can:

1. **Identify unmet needs:** Extreme users often have needs that are not adequately addressed by existing solutions in the market. Understanding their specific requirements can help you identify opportunities for innovation.
2. **Uncover workarounds and hacks:** Outliers may have developed their own workarounds or hacks to overcome the limitations of current offerings. These unconventional approaches can inspire new features, products, or services that cater to a broader audience.
3. **Anticipate future trends:** The behaviour and preferences of extreme users can often foreshadow future trends in the market. By observing how they interact with products or services, you can gain a glimpse into the direction the industry may be headed.

Techniques for Observing Extremes and Outliers:

1. **Ethnographic research:** Conduct in-depth, observational studies of extreme users in their natural environment. Watch how they interact with products or services, and look for patterns, frustrations, and unique adaptations.
2. **Interviews and focus groups:** Engage in one-on-one interviews or focus groups with extreme users and outliers. Ask open-ended questions to uncover their motivations, challenges, and desired outcomes.
3. **Social media listening:** Monitor social media platforms and online forums where extreme users and outliers congregate. Look for discussions about their experiences, modifications, and wishlist features.
4. **Lead user analysis:** Identify and collaborate with lead users – those who are at the forefront of the market and have already developed their own

solutions to unmet needs. They can provide valuable insights and ideas for disruptive innovation.

5. **Data analysis:** Analyze user data to identify patterns and anomalies that may indicate extreme behaviour or outlier preferences. Look for segments that deviate significantly from the norm in terms of usage, engagement, or outcomes.

GoPro

Before GoPro, the camera industry was primarily focused on serving the needs of mainstream consumers and professional photographers. Cameras were typically bulky, fragile, and not well-suited for capturing action-packed moments or outdoor adventures.

Identifying Extreme Users: GoPro's founder, Nick Woodman, was an avid surfer who wanted to capture his experiences on the waves. He realized that there was a gap in the market for a durable, portable, and easy-to-use camera that could withstand the rigours of extreme sports. Woodman identified surfers, snowboarders, skateboarders, and other action sports enthusiasts as extreme users who were underserved by traditional camera offerings.

Understanding the Needs of Extreme Users: Woodman and his team immersed themselves in the world of action sports to better understand the needs and pain points of these extreme users. They discovered that these individuals required:

1. **Durability:** A camera that could withstand harsh environments, shocks, and impacts.
2. **Portability:** A compact, lightweight camera that could be easily mounted on helmets, boards, or bodies.
3. **Ease of use:** A simple, intuitive camera that could be operated with one hand, even in challenging situations.
4. **Wide-angle lens:** A lens that could capture immersive, wide-angle

footage to convey the full experience of the action.

Developing a Solution: Based on these insights, GoPro developed its first camera, the 35mm HERO, which was a wrist-mounted, waterproof camera designed specifically for action sports. The camera's unique features, such as its compact size, rugged housing, and wide-angle lens, catered directly to the needs of extreme users.

Expanding the Market: As GoPro's popularity grew within the action sports community, the company realized that its cameras had appeal beyond just extreme users. By showcasing the incredible footage captured by these outliers, GoPro demonstrated the value of its cameras to a broader audience. The company expanded its marketing efforts to highlight the versatility of its cameras for capturing everyday adventures, travel experiences, and family moments.

Disrupting the Industry: GoPro's focus on the needs of extreme users and outliers allowed it to create a new category of cameras that disrupted the traditional camera industry. The company's cameras offered unique features and capabilities that were not available in mainstream offerings, such as:

1. **Mountable design:** GoPro's cameras could be easily attached to helmets, bikes, cars, and other objects, enabling users to capture footage from unique perspectives.
2. **Rugged durability:** The cameras were built to withstand extreme conditions, making them ideal for outdoor adventures and action sports.
3. **High-quality video:** Despite their compact size, GoPro's cameras offered high-quality video recording capabilities, allowing users to capture stunning footage.

By catering to the needs of extreme users and outliers, GoPro created a product that appealed to a wide range of consumers and disrupted the traditional camera market.

Slack

Before Slack, team communication and collaboration often relied on a patchwork of email, instant messaging, and project management tools. This fragmented approach led to information silos, lost context, and reduced productivity, particularly for teams working on complex, fast-paced projects.

Identifying Extreme Users: Slack's founders, Stewart Butterfield and Cal Henderson, were leading the development of a gaming company called Tiny Speck. As the team worked on their project, they found themselves struggling with the limitations of existing communication tools. The developers at Tiny Speck represented the extreme users who required a more streamlined, efficient, and context-rich way to collaborate.

Understanding the Needs of Extreme Users: The Slack team experienced firsthand the pain points and challenges faced by software developers and other tech-savvy teams. They identified several key needs:

1. **Centralized communication:** A single platform that could bring together all project-related communication, eliminating the need to switch between multiple tools.
2. **Contextual messaging:** The ability to organize conversations into topic-specific channels, making it easier to follow relevant discussions and maintain context.
3. **Seamless integration:** A platform that could easily integrate with the wide range of tools and services used by development teams, such as version control systems, bug trackers, and continuous integration platforms.
4. **Searchable history:** A searchable archive of all messages and files, allowing team members to quickly find and reference past discussions and decisions.

Developing a Solution: Butterfield and his team built an internal communication tool that addressed these specific needs. The tool, which eventually became Slack, offered a centralized platform for real-time messaging, organized conversations into channels, and provided robust search and integration capabilities. The team found that the tool significantly improved their own collaboration and productivity.

Expanding the Market: Recognizing the potential value of their internal tool, the Slack team decided to refine and release it as a standalone product. They initially targeted other software development teams, who shared similar communication challenges. As more teams adopted Slack and experienced its benefits, the company realized that the platform had broad appeal beyond just developers. Slack's user-friendly interface, customizable notifications, and wide range of integrations made it valuable for teams across various industries and functions.

Disrupting the Industry: Slack's focus on the needs of extreme users allowed it to create a product that disrupted the enterprise collaboration market. The platform offered several key advantages over traditional communication tools:

1. **Transparency and accessibility:** Slack's channel-based structure made communication more transparent and accessible to all team members, reducing information silos and improving collaboration.
2. **Customization and flexibility:** The platform's extensive integration capabilities and customizable notifications allowed teams to tailor Slack to their specific workflows and preferences.
3. **Improved productivity:** By centralizing communication, providing context-rich messaging, and enabling easy search and reference, Slack helped teams work more efficiently and effectively.

Slack's success in addressing the needs of extreme users and outliers led to rapid adoption and growth. The platform became the go-to communication tool for many startups, tech companies, and eventually, enterprises across various sectors. Slack's disruptive impact forced established players in the enterprise software market to rethink their offerings and adapt to the new expectations set by the platform.

Netflix

In the early days of Netflix, the company primarily focused on providing a wide selection of DVDs for rent through its mail-based subscription service. As the company transitioned to streaming video, it faced the challenge of understanding and catering to the diverse tastes of its growing subscriber base.

Identifying Outliers: Netflix recognized that while many of its users had mainstream viewing preferences, there were also outliers with unique, niche tastes in content. These outliers included viewers who were passionate about specific genres, subgenres, or even individual creators that were not well-represented in the mainstream media landscape.

Understanding the Needs of Outliers: Netflix leveraged its vast trove of user data to gain insights into the viewing habits and preferences of outliers. The company analyzed factors such as:

1. **Viewing history:** Netflix examined the specific titles, genres, and creators that outlier viewers watched, identifying patterns and commonalities.
2. **Engagement metrics:** The company studied how outlier viewers interacted with content, including factors such as completion rates, rewatching behavior, and ratings.
3. **Social sharing:** Netflix monitored how outlier viewers shared and discussed content on social media and other platforms, gauging their passion and enthusiasm for specific titles.

Through this analysis, Netflix discovered that outlier viewers were often underserved by traditional media outlets and were hungry for content that catered to their specific interests.

Developing a Solution: Armed with these insights, Netflix made a strategic decision to invest in original content that targeted the preferences of outlier viewers. The company used its data-driven understanding of outlier tastes to:

1. **Greenlight niche content:** Netflix commissioned original series, films, and documentaries that catered to specific genres, subcultures, and fan communities that were underrepresented in mainstream media.
2. **Personalize recommendations:** The company's sophisticated recommendation algorithms used the viewing data of outliers to suggest relevant, niche content to other users with similar tastes.
3. **Promote diverse voices:** Netflix actively sought out and supported creators from diverse backgrounds, giving a platform to unique perspectives and stories that resonated with outlier audiences.

Disrupting the Industry: By focusing on the needs of outlier viewers, Netflix disrupted the traditional media landscape in several key ways:

1. **Serving underrepresented audiences:** Netflix provided a home for niche content and diverse voices that were often overlooked by mainstream networks and studios.
2. **Creating cultural phenomena:** Some of Netflix's outlier-focused original content, such as "Stranger Things" and "Orange Is the New Black," became massive cultural hits, demonstrating the power of catering to specific audiences.
3. **Setting new standards:** Netflix's success with niche content forced other media companies to reassess their strategies and invest in more diverse, targeted programming.

Netflix's focus on outliers has had a significant impact on the media industry and popular culture. The company's success has paved the way for a more diverse, inclusive media landscape, where niche content and underrepresented voices can find a platform and an audience.

Moreover, Netflix's data-driven approach to understanding and serving outliers has become a model for other companies seeking to disrupt their industries. By leveraging data analytics to identify untapped market segments and develop tailored solutions, businesses can create products and services that resonate with specific audiences and drive growth.

In conclusion, observing the extremes and outliers within your target market can be a powerful source of inspiration for disruptive innovation. By understanding the unmet needs, unconventional behaviours, and unique adaptations of these individuals, you can identify opportunities for creating truly game-changing products or services. Embrace the insights gleaned from extreme users and outliers, and use them as a springboard for disrupting your industry and driving transformative growth.

＊＊

3

Targeting Next-Generation Customers

Disruptive innovation is a powerful strategy that enables companies to create new markets, reshape existing industries, and gain a competitive edge. While many organizations focus on improving their products and services to better serve their current customer base, a less explored but equally effective approach is to target next-generation customers. These potential customers have unique needs, preferences, and challenges that are not being adequately addressed by existing offerings in the market. By identifying and understanding these next-generation customers, companies can develop innovative solutions that disrupt the status quo and create new growth opportunities.

Identifying Next-Generation Customers: The first step in targeting next-generation customers is to identify who they are. Next-generation customers may belong to a different demographic, have different lifestyles, or face unique challenges compared to a company's existing customer base. To identify potential next-generation customers, companies must conduct thorough market research, observe various customer segments, and analyze their behaviour and preferences. This process may involve looking beyond the company's traditional target market and considering new customer segments that have been previously overlooked or underserved.

Understanding the Needs of Next-Generation Customers: Once potential next-generation customers have been identified, companies must gain a deep understanding of their needs, fears, aspirations, and pain points. This requires a combination of qualitative and quantitative research methods, such as observations, interviews, surveys, and data analysis. By immersing themselves in the lives of next-generation customers, companies can uncover unmet needs, identify gaps in the market, and spot opportunities for innovation. Understanding the unique challenges and desires of these customers is crucial for developing products and services that resonate with them and address their specific needs.

Assessing the Market Potential: Before investing in the development of new products or services targeted at next-generation customers, companies must assess the market potential. This involves evaluating factors such as the size of the target market, the willingness of customers to pay for solutions that meet their needs, and the potential for long-term growth and profitability. Assessing the market potential helps companies determine whether targeting next-generation customers is a viable strategy and ensures that resources are allocated effectively.

Developing Innovative Solutions: Armed with a deep understanding of next-generation customers and a clear assessment of the market potential, companies can focus on developing innovative solutions that address the specific needs and pain points of these customers. This may involve creating entirely new products or services, or adapting existing offerings to better suit the preferences of the target market. The key is to develop solutions that are differentiated, relevant, and valuable to next-generation customers, offering them a compelling reason to choose the company's products or services over those of competitors.

Marketing and Engaging Next-Generation Customers: Successfully targeting next-generation customers requires more than just developing innovative products or services. Companies must also effectively market and engage these customers to build awareness, generate interest, and foster loyalty. This may involve using different communication channels, messaging strategies, and engagement tactics compared to those used for existing customers. By tailoring their marketing efforts to the preferences and behaviors of next-generation customers, companies can effectively reach and resonate with this new target market.

Dollar Shave Club

Dollar Shave Club (DSC) is a subscription-based razor and men's grooming company that created disruptive innovation by targeting next-generation customers in the traditional razor industry.

Identifying Next-Generation Customers: DSC identified a new potential customer segment: younger, tech-savvy men who were frustrated with the high costs and inconvenience of purchasing razors through traditional retail channels. These next-generation customers were more open to online shopping and subscription-based services, and they valued simplicity, convenience, and affordability in their grooming products.

Understanding the Needs of Next-Generation Customers: DSC recognized that their target customers were dissatisfied with the expensive, overdesigned razors marketed by established brands like Gillette. They understood that these next-generation customers wanted a simple, high-quality razor at a reasonable price, delivered directly to their doorstep without the hassle of shopping in stores. DSC also realized that its target customers valued humour, irreverence, and authenticity in brand communication.

Developing Innovative Solutions: Based on their understanding of next-generation customers, DSC developed a subscription-based service that delivered high-quality, low-cost razors directly to customers' doors on a monthly basis. They offered a simple selection of razors, focusing on quality rather than gimmicky features. DSC also expanded their product line to include other men's grooming essentials, such as shave butter, body wash, and hair styling products, to meet the broader needs of their target customers.

Marketing and Engaging Next-Generation Customers: DSC's marketing strategy was tailored to appeal to their next-generation customer segment. The company created humorous, edgy online videos that poked fun at the pretentiousness of established razor brands and highlighted the simplicity and affordability of DSC's products. These videos went viral, generating millions of views and creating a buzz around the brand. DSC also leveraged social media to engage with their customers, fostering a sense of community and brand loyalty.

Impact and Disruption: Dollar Shave Club's innovative approach successfully disrupted the razor industry, capturing a significant market share and forcing established players like Gillette to reevaluate their strategies. In just five years, DSC grew to a valuation of $1 billion and was eventually acquired by Unilever for $1 billion in 2016. The company's success demonstrates the power of targeting next-generation customers and creating innovative solutions that address their unique needs and preferences.

Impossible Foods

Impossible Foods is a food technology company that created disruptive innovation in the food industry by targeting next-generation customers with their plant-based meat alternatives.

Identifying Next-Generation Customers: Impossible Foods identified a growing segment of consumers, particularly younger generations, who were concerned about the environmental impact, animal welfare issues, and health consequences associated with traditional meat consumption. These next-generation customers were more open to trying plant-based alternatives and were actively seeking out more sustainable and ethical food options.

Understanding the Needs of Next-Generation Customers: Impossible Foods recognized that their target customers wanted plant-based meat alternatives that closely mimicked the taste, texture, and overall experience of consuming real meat. They understood that these next-generation customers were unwilling to compromise on taste and satisfaction, even as they sought out more sustainable and ethical food choices. Additionally, these customers valued transparency and authenticity in the brands they supported.

Developing Innovative Solutions: Based on their understanding of next-generation customers, Impossible Foods developed a range of plant-based meat products, including the Impossible Burger, which was designed to look, cook, and taste like traditional ground beef. The company's innovative use of ingredients like soy leghemoglobin allowed them to recreate the flavour and aroma of real meat, appealing to the preferences of their target customers. Impossible Foods also focused on making their products widely available through partnerships with restaurants, fast-food chains, and grocery stores, ensuring that their plant-based meat alternatives were accessible to a broad range of consumers.

Marketing and Engaging Next-Generation Customers: Impossible Foods' marketing strategy focused on highlighting the environmental benefits and ethical advantages of their plant-based meat products, which resonated with their next-generation customer segment. The company participated in high-profile events, such as the Consumer Electronics Show (CES), to showcase its innovative products and generate buzz among tech-savvy consumers. Impossible Foods also leveraged social media and influencer partnerships to spread awareness and engage with their target customers, fostering a sense of community around their brand and mission.

Impact and Disruption: Impossible Foods' plant-based meat alternatives have disrupted the traditional meat industry, forcing established players to take notice and develop their own plant-based offerings. The company's success has also inspired a wave of innovation and investment in the plant-based food sector, with numerous startups and established food companies following in their footsteps. Impossible Foods' disruptive innovation has not only appealed to next-generation customers but has also contributed to a broader shift in consumer preferences towards more sustainable and ethical food choices.

In conclusion, targeting next-generation customers is a powerful strategy for creating disruptive innovation and driving growth. By identifying potential next-generation customers, understanding their unique needs and preferences, assessing the market potential, developing innovative solutions, and effectively marketing and engaging these customers, companies can unlock new opportunities and gain a competitive advantage. While this approach requires a significant investment of time, resources, and effort, the rewards can be substantial, enabling companies to create new markets, disrupt existing industries, and achieve long-term success.

* * *

4

Anticipate Future Trends/Needs

One of the most powerful ways to create disruptive innovation is by anticipating future trends and customer needs before they become mainstream. This allows companies to get ahead of the curve and introduce groundbreaking products, services, or business models that reshape industries. However, predicting the future is inherently challenging and requires a thoughtful approach.

Analyze Social, Technological, and Economic Shifts: The first step in anticipating future trends is to carefully study the major social, technological, and economic forces that are transforming the world. This could include:

- Demographic shifts like population aging in developed countries and the rise of the middle class in emerging markets
- The growing impact of digital technologies like AI, blockchain, IoT, etc. across industries
- Changes in economic conditions, globalization, trade flows, and consumption patterns
- The increasing importance of sustainability, ethics, and purpose-driven business

By tracking these macro forces, companies can identify potential discontinuities that could enable disruptive innovations. For example, the sharing economy emerged at the intersection of digital platforms, urban population density, and a new generation that prioritized access over ownership.

Envision Alternative Futures: Based on the key trends identified, companies should envision a range of plausible future scenarios, from incremental shifts to radical transformations. This futures thinking approach, pioneered by Shell and other companies, helps break linear thinking and explore a wider solution space.

For each scenario, consider how customer needs, industry dynamics, and the basis of competition could fundamentally change. What new problems will customers face? Which pain points will become more acute? How could value chains be reshaped? The goal is to uncover latent needs and spot untapped innovation opportunities.

Engage Lead Users and Extreme Customers: To develop a deeper understanding of emerging needs, companies should engage lead users and customers at the extremes. As MIT professor Eric von Hippel has shown, lead users often pioneer novel solutions because they experience needs ahead of the mainstream market. Extreme users like customers in emerging markets or those with disabilities also have unique needs that can spur inclusive innovations.

Companies should collaborate closely with these pioneering customers to gain early insights into unmet needs and co-create solutions. The risk is that their needs may seem too niche at first. But as Facebook's early focus on college students and Airbnb's initial appeal to couch-surfing enthusiasts show, a compelling innovation for extreme users can ultimately spread to the mass market.

Conduct Rapid Experiments: Finally, to stay ahead of fast-moving trends, companies need to adopt a rapid experimentation mindset. Rather than over-analyzing the future, they should place small bets on promising opportunities, learn from real customer feedback, and adapt quickly. Alibaba's Hema grocery stores, Amazon Go, and the Amazon Dash button are all examples of rapid experiments to test new retail concepts.

By running multiple experiments across different time horizons, companies can maintain a pipeline of near-term and long-term innovation opportunities. The key is to foster a culture of continuous learning, maintain strategic flexibility, and be willing to pivot as the future unfolds in unexpected ways.

Samsung Foldable Smartphones

Samsung recognized the growing demand for larger screen sizes and the potential of flexible display technology to enable new form factors. They anticipated that consumers would want the benefits of a larger screen for immersive media consumption, multitasking, and productivity while maintaining the portability and convenience of a smaller device.

By developing foldable OLED displays and hinge mechanisms, Samsung introduced the Galaxy Fold and Galaxy Z Flip smartphones, which offer a transformative experience. These devices combine the functionality of a tablet and a smartphone in a single, pocketable device, meeting the needs of users who want the best of both worlds.

The Galaxy Fold features a large, 7.3-inch foldable display that allows users to seamlessly switch between a compact phone mode and an expansive tablet mode. This innovative design enables new use cases, such as running multiple apps simultaneously, viewing content on a larger screen, and enhancing productivity on the go. The Galaxy Z Flip, on the other hand, offers a more compact clamshell design that fits easily in a pocket or purse, while still providing a full-sized smartphone experience when unfolded.

By anticipating the need for more screen real estate and the potential of flexible displays, Samsung disrupted the smartphone market and introduced a new category of devices. They recognized that incremental improvements in specs and features were no longer enough to excite consumers and that a fundamental rethinking of the smartphone form factor was necessary.

Samsung's foldable smartphones also anticipated the growing importance

ANTICIPATE FUTURE TRENDS/NEEDS

of multitasking and productivity on mobile devices. With the ability to run multiple apps side-by-side, view content on a larger screen, and use the device in various modes, foldable smartphones meet the needs of users who increasingly rely on their mobile devices for work and creative tasks.

Furthermore, Samsung anticipated the need for a premium, differentiated experience in the mature smartphone market. By offering cutting-edge technology, innovative design, and a new form factor, Samsung's foldable smartphones create a sense of exclusivity and novelty that appeals to early adopters and tech enthusiasts.

While foldable smartphones are still a nascent category with challenges to overcome, such as durability and affordability, Samsung's early investments in this technology demonstrate their ability to anticipate future trends and needs. As foldable displays become more refined and mainstream, Samsung is well-positioned to lead this new segment and shape the future of mobile computing.

Casper Mattresses

Casper recognized the growing frustration with the traditional mattress shopping experience, which often involved high-pressure sales tactics, confusing options, and inconvenient delivery and setup processes. They anticipated the need for a simpler, more transparent, and customer-centric approach to buying mattresses, particularly among younger, digitally-savvy consumers.

By offering a streamlined product line, online-only purchasing, and free shipping and returns, Casper disrupted the mattress industry and met the evolving needs of consumers. They recognized the potential of e-commerce and DTC business models to transform the way people shop for large, considered purchases like mattresses.

Casper's innovative approach anticipated several key trends and needs in the mattress market:

1. **Convenience:** Casper anticipated the demand for a more convenient mattress buying experience, eliminating the need to visit physical stores and deal with salespeople. By offering online ordering, free shipping, and a 100-night trial period, Casper made it easy for customers to purchase a mattress from the comfort of their homes and try it out risk-free.
2. **Simplicity:** Casper recognized the need for a simpler, less overwhelming mattress buying process. By offering a single, universally comfortable mattress model (at least initially), Casper reduced decision fatigue and made it easy for customers to choose the right product for their needs.
3. **Affordability:** Casper anticipated the demand for high-quality mattresses at more affordable prices. By cutting out middlemen and selling directly to consumers, Casper was able to offer premium mattresses at lower prices than traditional retailers, meeting the needs of budget-conscious shoppers.
4. **Brand experience:** Casper recognized the growing importance of brand experience and customer engagement in the mattress industry. By creating a strong brand identity, using engaging content marketing, and leveraging social media, Casper built a loyal community of customers and advocated around the importance of sleep and wellness.
5. **Packaging and setup:** Casper anticipated the need for a more seamless delivery and setup experience. By compressing their mattresses into **compact, easy-to-maneuver boxes** and offering simple, tool-free setup, Casper made it convenient for customers to receive and install their new mattresses without the hassle of traditional delivery methods.

By anticipating these trends and needs, Casper disrupted the traditional mattress industry and paved the way for a new wave of DTC mattress startups. They recognized that consumers were ready for a new approach to mattress shopping that prioritized convenience, simplicity, affordability, and customer experience.

In summary, anticipating future trends and needs is a critical strategy for driving disruptive innovation. Companies can uncover game-changing

ANTICIPATE FUTURE TRENDS/NEEDS

opportunities ahead of their competitors by analyzing social and technological shifts, envisioning alternative futures, collaborating with lead users, and conducting rapid experiments. As the old Wayne Gretzky adage goes, "Skate to where the puck is going, not where it has been."

* * *

5

Democratizing Access

Disruptive innovation often stems from identifying opportunities to make products or services that were previously accessible only to a skilled or affluent segment of the population available to a broader, less privileged market. By democratizing access to these exclusive offerings, companies can create new markets, tap into unmet needs, and drive significant growth and impact.

The Power of Democratizing Access

Historically, many products and services have been limited to those with the means, skills, or resources to access them. This exclusivity can be due to factors such as high costs, complex technology, or required expertise. However, by finding ways to make these offerings more affordable, user-friendly, or convenient, companies can open up new markets and create disruptive innovations that transform industries.

Strategies for Democratizing Access:

1. **Simplification:** One approach to democratizing access is to simplify complex products or services, making them easier for a broader audience to understand and use. This can involve streamlining features, creating

intuitive interfaces, or providing guided experiences that reduce the need for specialized knowledge.
2. **Cost Reduction:** Another strategy is to find ways to reduce the cost of producing or delivering a product or service, making it more affordable for a wider range of consumers. This can be achieved through technological advancements, economies of scale, or innovative business models that reduce overhead and pass savings on to customers.
3. **Convenience:** Making products or services more convenient and accessible is another way to democratize access. This can involve offering online or mobile platforms, providing home delivery, or creating self-service options that eliminate the need for intermediaries or specialized assistance.
4. **Education and Empowerment:** Democratizing access can also involve providing educational resources or tools that empower users to engage with products or services that were previously out of reach. This can include tutorials, community forums, or user-friendly guides that help people navigate complex topics or technologies.

Examples of Disruptive Innovations through Democratizing Access:

1. **Personal Computers:** Before the advent of personal computers, computing technology was primarily accessible to large corporations, government agencies, and research institutions. Companies like Apple and Microsoft democratized access to computing by creating affordable, user-friendly PCs that could be used by individuals and small businesses.
2. **Online Learning Platforms:** Traditionally, access to high-quality education was limited to those who could afford to attend prestigious universities or had the time and resources to pursue in-person learning. Online learning platforms like Coursera and edX have democratized access to education by offering affordable, flexible courses to learners worldwide from top institutions.
3. **Robo-advisors:** Financial advice and investment management services have historically been accessible mainly to wealthy individuals who could

afford to hire professional advisors. Robo-advisors like Betterment and Wealthfront have democratized access to these services by using algorithms to provide low-cost, automated investment advice to a broader range of consumers.

4. **Telemedicine:** Access to healthcare has often been limited by factors such as geography, cost, and availability of specialists. Telemedicine platforms like Teladoc and Doctor on Demand have democratized access to medical care by allowing patients to consult with doctors remotely, reducing barriers to treatment and improving convenience.

Implementing a Democratizing Access Strategy: To successfully democratize access to a product or service, companies should consider the following steps:

1. **Identify Exclusivity:** Analyze the market to identify products, services, or experiences that are currently accessible only to a limited segment of the population due to factors like cost, complexity, or required expertise.
2. **Understand Barriers:** Investigate the specific barriers that prevent broader access to these offerings, such as high prices, technical complexity, or lack of awareness.
3. **Develop Solutions:** Brainstorm and prototype solutions that address these barriers, focusing on strategies like simplification, cost reduction, convenience, or education.
4. **Test and Refine:** Pilot the solutions with a target audience, gathering feedback and data to refine and improve the offering.
5. **Scale and Promote:** Once the solution has been validated, develop a go-to-market strategy to scale the offering and promote it to the broader target market, emphasizing the benefits of increased access and convenience.

Warby Parker

Before Warby Parker, the eyewear industry was dominated by a few large companies that kept prices high and limited consumer choice. Prescription glasses were often expensive, with prices ranging from $300 to $800 or more. Many consumers found it difficult to afford quality eyewear, and the buying process was often inconvenient, requiring visits to optometrists and optical shops.

Identifying the Opportunity: Warby Parker's founders, Neil Blumenthal, Andrew Hunt, David Gilboa, and Jeffrey Raider, saw an opportunity to democratize access to prescription eyewear by offering stylish, high-quality glasses at a fraction of the traditional cost. They recognized that by cutting out middlemen and designing glasses in-house, they could significantly reduce prices while still providing a great product and customer experience.

Developing the Solution: Warby Parker developed a vertically integrated business model that allowed them to control every aspect of the eyewear production and distribution process. They designed their own frames, sourced materials directly from suppliers, and sold glasses online and through their own retail stores.

Key Aspects of Warby Parker's Democratizing Access Strategy:

1. **Affordability:** By cutting out middlemen and selling directly to consumers, Warby Parker was able to offer prescription glasses at a much lower price point than traditional retailers, typically $95 including lenses.
2. **Convenience:** Warby Parker's online platform made it easy for customers to browse styles, select frames, and upload their prescription information. They also offered a home try-on program, allowing customers to choose up to five frames to try on at home for free before making a purchase.
3. **Style and Quality:** Despite their lower prices, Warby Parker focused on offering stylish, high-quality frames that appealed to fashion-conscious consumers. They invested in design and materials to ensure that their

glasses were both attractive and durable.
4. **Social Impact:** Warby Parker also incorporated a social mission into its business model, partnering with nonprofits to distribute a pair of glasses to someone in need for every pair sold. This "Buy a Pair, Give a Pair" program helped to further democratize access to eyewear in underserved communities worldwide.

Impact and Disruption: Warby Parker's democratizing access strategy had a significant impact on the eyewear industry:

1. **Market Expansion:** By offering affordable, stylish prescription glasses, Warby Parker made it possible for more people to access quality eyewear, expanding the overall market for prescription glasses.
2. **Increased Competition:** Warby Parker's success challenged traditional eyewear retailers to reconsider their pricing and business models, leading to increased competition and more choices for consumers.
3. **Omnichannel Retailing:** While initially an online-only retailer, Warby Parker eventually expanded into brick-and-mortar stores, demonstrating the value of an omnichannel approach that combines online convenience with in-person service and support.
4. **Inspirational Branding:** Warby Parker's branding, which emphasized value, good design, and social impact, struck a chord with millennials and other socially conscious consumers, demonstrating the power of aligning the brand with consumer values.

By identifying an opportunity to make stylish, high-quality prescription glasses more affordable and accessible, Warby Parker created a disruptive innovation that transformed the eyewear industry.

Square

Before Square, accepting credit card payments was often difficult and expensive for small businesses and entrepreneurs. Traditional payment processors charged high fees, required lengthy applications, and often imposed minimum sales volumes. As a result, many small businesses were unable to accept credit cards, limiting their growth potential and putting them at a disadvantage compared to larger competitors.

Identifying the Opportunity: Square's co-founders, Jack Dorsey and Jim McKelvey, saw an opportunity to democratize access to payment processing by creating a simple, affordable, and accessible solution for small businesses. They recognized that by leveraging mobile technology and streamlining the onboarding process, they could empower entrepreneurs to accept credit card payments and manage their businesses more effectively.

Developing the Solution: Square developed a compact credit card reader that could be plugged into a smartphone or tablet, allowing businesses to accept payments anywhere. They also created a user-friendly app that made it easy for businesses to track sales, manage inventory, and send invoices.

Key Aspects of Square's Democratizing Access Strategy:

1. **Affordability:** Square offered a simple, transparent pricing model with no monthly fees and a low, flat rate per transaction. This made payment processing accessible to businesses of all sizes, even those with low sales volumes.
2. **Ease of Use:** Square's credit card reader and app were designed to be user-friendly and intuitive, requiring no technical expertise to set up and use. This made it easy for entrepreneurs to start accepting payments quickly and manage their businesses on the go.
3. **Accessibility:** By leveraging mobile technology, Square made payment processing accessible to businesses that previously could not accept credit cards, such as food trucks, farmers market vendors, and mobile service providers.
4. **Ecosystem Expansion:** Over time, Square expanded its ecosystem to

include additional tools and services, such as inventory management, employee management, and small business loans, further democratizing access to essential business management resources.

Impact and Disruption: Square's democratizing access strategy had a profound impact on the payment processing industry and the small business landscape:

1. **Market Expansion:** By making payment processing affordable and accessible, Square opened up new growth opportunities for small businesses and entrepreneurs, allowing them to compete more effectively with larger companies.
2. **Industry Transformation:** Square's success challenged traditional payment processors to simplify their pricing models and improve their user experiences, leading to increased competition and innovation in the industry.
3. **Economic Empowerment:** By empowering small businesses and entrepreneurs to accept credit card payments and manage their businesses more effectively, Square helped to level the playing field and support economic growth at the grassroots level.
4. **Ecosystem Development:** Square's expanding ecosystem of business management tools and services created a comprehensive platform for small businesses, further democratizing access to resources that were previously out of reach for many entrepreneurs.

Square's democratizing access strategy demonstrates the power of leveraging technology to make essential business tools and services more affordable, accessible, and user-friendly.

In conclusion, democratizing access to exclusive products and services can be a powerful strategy for creating disruptive innovations that transform industries and improve people's lives. By identifying opportunities to make these offerings more affordable, user-friendly, or convenient, companies can tap into new markets, meet unmet needs, and drive significant growth and impact. As technology continues to advance and consumer expectations evolve, the potential for democratizing access will only continue to grow, presenting endless opportunities for innovative companies to create value and disrupt the status quo.

* * *

6

Reimagining Customer Experience

One powerful strategy for driving disruptive innovation is to reimagine the customer experience. By fundamentally rethinking how customers interact with and derive value from a company's offerings, businesses can create entirely new markets, differentiate themselves from competitors, and establish long-term customer loyalty.

Understanding Customer Experience: Customer experience encompasses the entire journey that a customer goes through when interacting with a company, from initial awareness and consideration to purchase, use, and post-purchase support. It includes all touchpoints, interactions, and emotions that a customer experiences along the way. A positive customer experience is essential for building brand loyalty, driving word-of-mouth referrals, and, ultimately, achieving business success.

However, in many industries, the customer experience has remained largely unchanged for decades, with companies focusing on incremental improvements rather than fundamental reimagination. This creates an opportunity for disruptive innovation by companies that are willing to challenge the status quo and rethink the customer experience from the ground up.

Identifying Customer Pain Points and Unmet Needs: The first step in reimagining the customer experience is to gain a deep understanding of the pain points, frustrations, and unmet needs that customers face in a particular industry or market. This requires a combination of customer research, observation, and empathy. Some key methods for identifying customer pain points and unmet needs include:

1. Customer interviews and focus groups
2. Ethnographic research and observation
3. Customer journey mapping
4. Social media listening and sentiment analysis
5. Analyzing customer feedback and complaints

By gathering insights from these sources, companies can identify areas where the current customer experience falls short and opportunities for creating a differentiated, superior experience.

Reimagining the End-to-End Customer Journey: Once customer pain points and unmet needs have been identified, the next step is to reimagine the entire end-to-end customer journey. This involves looking beyond individual touchpoints and interactions and instead considering how all aspects of the customer experience can be redesigned to create a seamless, intuitive, and delightful journey.

Some key principles for reimagining the customer journey include:

1. **Simplicity:** Streamlining processes, reducing friction, and making it easy for customers to achieve their goals.
2. **Personalization:** Tailoring the experience to individual customer preferences, needs, and contexts.
3. **Convenience:** Providing options and flexibility that fit seamlessly into customers' lives and routines.
4. **Emotional connection:** Creating experiences that resonate emotionally and build long-term customer relationships.
5. **Consistency:** Ensuring that the customer experience is consistent and cohesive across all touchpoints and interactions.

By applying these principles and thinking creatively about how the customer experience can be reimagined, companies can develop innovative solutions that set them apart from competitors and create new market opportunities.

Leveraging Technology to Enable Disruptive Customer Experiences: Technology can be a powerful enabler of disruptive customer experiences. By leveraging emerging technologies such as artificial intelligence, the Internet of Things, virtual and augmented reality, and blockchain, companies can create experiences that were previously impossible or impractical.

For example, artificial intelligence can be used to personalize recommendations, anticipate customer needs, and provide proactive support. The Internet of Things can enable connected, context-aware experiences that adapt to customers' changing needs and preferences. Virtual and augmented reality can create immersive, engaging experiences that blur the line between the physical and digital worlds. Blockchain can enable secure, transparent, and decentralized transactions and interactions.

The key is to focus on how these technologies can be applied to solve real customer problems and create value in new and innovative ways, rather than simply adopting technology for its own sake.

Continuously Iterating and Improving: Creating disruptive innovation through reimagined customer experiences is not a one-time event, but an ongoing process of continuous iteration and improvement. As customer needs and preferences evolve, and as new technologies emerge, companies must continually reassess and refine their approach to the customer experience.

This requires a culture of customer-centricity, experimentation, and learning. Companies must be willing to take risks, test new ideas, and learn from both successes and failures. They must also have processes in place for gathering and acting on customer feedback, and for rapidly iterating and improving based on that feedback.

Amazon

Amazon, founded by Jeff Bezos in 1994, started as an online bookstore but quickly expanded to become one of the world's largest and most influential retailers. At the heart of Amazon's success is its relentless focus on reimagining the customer experience. By fundamentally rethinking how customers shop and interact with a retail brand, Amazon has created a disruptive innovation that has transformed the retail industry and raised the bar for customer experience across sectors.

One-Click Ordering and Fast, Free Shipping: One of Amazon's earliest innovations was the introduction of one-click ordering, which allows customers to make a purchase with a single click, without having to repeatedly enter their shipping and payment information. This simple but powerful feature removes friction from the purchasing process and makes it incredibly easy and convenient for customers to buy products online.

In addition to one-click ordering, Amazon has continually pushed the boundaries of fast and free shipping. With the introduction of Amazon Prime in 2005, the company began offering free two-day shipping to members for an annual fee. Over time, Amazon has expanded Prime to include same-day and even one-hour delivery options in select markets. By making fast and free shipping the norm, Amazon has fundamentally changed customer expectations for online retail and forced competitors to follow suit.

Personalized Recommendations: Another key aspect of Amazon's reimagined customer experience is its use of personalized recommendations. By leveraging the vast amounts of data it collects on customer browsing and purchase behaviour, Amazon is able to provide highly relevant product recommendations to each individual customer. These recommendations appear throughout the shopping experience, from the homepage to product detail pages to post-purchase follow-up emails.

Personalized recommendations not only help customers discover new products they might be interested in but also create a sense of personalization and emotional connection. Customers feel like Amazon understands their needs and preferences, and is actively working to help them find the right products. This level of personalization has become a key differentiator for Amazon and has been widely imitated by other retailers.

Customer Reviews and Ratings: Amazon was one of the first online retailers to allow customers to leave reviews and ratings for products. This feature has become a critical part of the Amazon shopping experience, providing social proof and helping customers make informed purchase decisions. Customer reviews and ratings also serve as a form of user-generated content, which can improve a product's search rankings and visibility on the site.

In addition to displaying customer reviews and ratings, Amazon uses this data to inform its personalized recommendations and search results. Products with higher ratings and more positive reviews are more likely to be recommended to customers and to appear at the top of search results. This creates a virtuous cycle, where highly-rated products become even more visible and popular over time.

Proactive Customer Support: Amazon has also reimagined customer support by leveraging technology to anticipate and address customer needs before they even arise. For example, the company uses machine learning algorithms to predict when a customer may need help with a product and proactively reaches out with support resources and recommendations.

Amazon has also introduced innovative support channels like chatbots and voice assistants (e.g., Amazon Alexa), which allow customers to get help and support in more natural and conversational ways. These tools use natural language processing and machine learning to understand customer queries and provide relevant, personalized responses.

Continuous Innovation: Perhaps most importantly, Amazon has a culture of continuous experimentation and innovation when it comes to the customer experience. The company is constantly testing new ideas and features, from small tweaks to the website design to major new initiatives like Amazon Go (cashierless physical stores) and Amazon Alexa (voice-powered virtual assistant).

This culture of innovation is driven by a focus on long-term customer value rather than short-term profits. Amazon is willing to invest heavily in new technologies and business models that have the potential to create a better customer experience, even if they don't pay off immediately. This long-term orientation has allowed Amazon to stay ahead of the curve and continue disrupting the retail industry year after year.

Through its relentless focus on reimagining the customer experience, Amazon has become one of the most valuable and influential companies in the world. Its innovations have not only disrupted traditional retail but have also set new standards for customer experience across industries.

Uber

Uber, founded in 2009, is a transportation network company that has revolutionized the way people commute and travel. By reimagining the customer experience in the transportation industry, Uber has created a disruptive innovation that has challenged traditional taxi services and transformed urban mobility.

Convenient and Cashless Rides: One of the key aspects of Uber's reimagined customer experience is the convenience and simplicity of requesting and paying for rides. With just a few taps on a smartphone app, customers can request a ride, see the estimated time of arrival, and track the driver's location in real-time. This level of transparency and control was previously unheard of in the traditional taxi industry.

Moreover, Uber rides are entirely cashless. Customers link their credit card or other payment method to their Uber account, and the fare is automatically charged at the end of the ride. This eliminates the need for cash transactions and the potential for disputes over fares or change. The cashless experience is not only more convenient for customers but also safer for drivers.

Personalized and Flexible Ride Options: Another key aspect of Uber's customer experience is the personalization and flexibility of ride options. Uber offers a range of ride types to suit different customer needs and preferences, from budget-friendly UberPOOL (shared rides) to premium UberBLACK (luxury vehicles with professional drivers).

Customers can also personalize their ride experience by specifying preferences such as the vehicle size, the driver's language, or even the preferred temperature of the car. This level of customization makes the Uber experience feel tailored to each individual customer's needs.

Dynamic Pricing and Demand Management: Uber has also introduced innovative pricing and demand management features that optimize the customer experience. The most well-known of these is surge pricing, where ride prices increase during periods of high demand to incentivize more drivers to come online and ensure ride availability for customers.

While surge pricing has sometimes been controversial, it reflects Uber's commitment to using technology and data to dynamically match supply and demand and ensure a reliable customer experience. Uber also uses machine learning algorithms to predict demand patterns and proactively encourage drivers to be available in high-demand areas and times.

Seamless Multimodal Integration: More recently, Uber has begun to reimagine urban mobility more broadly by integrating multiple modes of transportation into its platform. In addition to ride-hailing, Uber now offers bike and scooter rentals, public transit ticketing, and even helicopter rides in some markets.

By integrating these different transportation modes into a single, seamless customer experience, Uber is making it easier for customers to navigate cities and choose the best transportation option for their needs. This multimodal integration represents a significant expansion of Uber's value proposition and a reimagination of how customers interact with urban transportation systems.

Continuous Innovation and Expansion: Like Amazon, Uber has a culture of continuous innovation and is constantly experimenting with new features and services to enhance the customer experience. For example, Uber has introduced features like in-app messaging to facilitate communication between drivers and riders, and Uber Eats for food delivery.

Uber has also aggressively expanded into new markets around the world, adapting its service to local conditions and customer preferences. This global expansion has allowed Uber to scale its reimagined customer experience and disrupt transportation industries worldwide.

Uber's reimagination of the transportation customer experience has had a profound impact on urban mobility and has sparked a wave of similar innovations in the transportation sector. Its success demonstrates the power of reimagining customer experience to create disruptive innovation, even in traditional, heavily-regulated industries.

Reimagining the customer experience is a powerful strategy for creating disruptive innovation. By gaining a deep understanding of customer pain points and unmet needs, reimagining the end-to-end customer journey, leveraging technology to enable new experiences, and continuously iterating and improving, companies can create differentiated, superior experiences that set them apart from competitors and drive long-term growth and success. As the brand examples demonstrate, the rewards of this approach can be significant, not only for individual companies but for entire industries and markets.

* * *

7

Simplifying Customer Journeys

Disruptive innovation is often associated with groundbreaking technologies or radical business models. However, one of the most effective ways to create disruptive innovation is by simplifying customer journeys and reducing the number of steps required to achieve a goal. By streamlining processes and eliminating unnecessary complexity, companies can create products and services that fundamentally transform the customer experience and disrupt entire industries.

The Power of Simplification

In today's fast-paced world, customers value convenience, efficiency, and ease of use. They want products and services that help them achieve their goals quickly and with minimal effort. Companies that can deliver on these expectations by simplifying customer journeys have a significant competitive advantage.

Simplification involves identifying the key steps in a customer's journey and finding ways to reduce or eliminate unnecessary complexity. This can involve:

1. **Reducing the number of steps:** By minimizing the number of steps

required to complete a task, companies can make their products or services more efficient and user-friendly.
2. **Eliminating friction points:** Friction points are moments in the customer journey that cause frustration, confusion, or delays. By identifying and eliminating these friction points, companies can create a smoother, more seamless experience.
3. **Automating processes:** Automation can help reduce the time and effort required to complete certain tasks, making the overall journey more efficient and convenient for customers.
4. **Integrating systems:** By integrating different systems and platforms, companies can create a more unified and streamlined experience for customers, reducing the need for manual intervention or switching between multiple tools.

The Benefits of Simplification

Simplifying customer journeys can lead to several benefits for both customers and companies:

1. **Improved customer satisfaction:** When customers can achieve their goals quickly and easily, they are more likely to be satisfied with the overall experience. This can lead to increased loyalty, positive word-of-mouth, and repeat business.
2. **Increased adoption and usage:** Products and services that are easy to use and require fewer steps are more likely to be adopted and used regularly by customers. This can lead to higher engagement, retention, and revenue growth.
3. **Differentiation from competitors:** By offering a simpler, more streamlined experience than competitors, companies can differentiate themselves in the market and attract customers who value convenience and ease of use.
4. **Cost savings:** Simplifying processes and reducing complexity can also lead to cost savings for companies, as they can eliminate unnecessary

steps, automate tasks, and reduce the need for customer support.

Simplification as a Disruptive Force

When taken to an extreme, simplification can be a powerful force for disruptive innovation. By fundamentally reimagining how a product or service is delivered and consumed, companies can create entirely new markets or disrupt existing industries.

For example, the introduction of ride-sharing services like Uber and Lyft disrupted the traditional taxi industry by simplifying the process of hailing a ride. Instead of calling a dispatcher, waiting for a cab, and paying with cash, customers could now request a ride, track its arrival, and pay electronically, all through a simple smartphone app. This simplification of the customer journey made ride-sharing more convenient, accessible, and affordable than traditional taxis, leading to rapid adoption and industry disruption.

Similarly, the rise of streaming services like Netflix and Spotify disrupted the entertainment industry by simplifying the process of accessing and consuming media content. Instead of purchasing individual movies or albums, customers could now access vast libraries of content through a single, easy-to-use platform, with personalized recommendations and seamless playback across devices. This simplification of the media consumption journey transformed the way people watch movies and listen to music, disrupting traditional business models in the process.

Apple's iPod and iTunes

Apple's introduction of the iPod and iTunes in the early 2000s is a prime example of how simplifying customer journeys can lead to disruptive innovation.

Before the iPod, the process of downloading and listening to digital music was cumbersome and time-consuming. Users had to:

1. Switch on their computer and open a web browser

2. Search for a song, often taking considerable time to locate it
3. If the song was available for preview, listen to it on the computer
4. If the song was not satisfactory, start the search process again
5. If the song was good, search again for a place to download it (often resorting to piracy due to limited legal options)
6. Download the song, which could take several minutes depending on internet speeds
7. Repeat the process for each song, spending hours collecting music
8. Transfer the songs to an MP3 player, which often had a clunky interface and limited storage capacity
9. Organize the music collection on the MP3 player, which could be difficult and time-consuming
10. Navigate the MP3 player's complex interface to find and play the desired song

This complex and fragmented process made it difficult for users to enjoy a seamless, user-friendly music experience.

Apple's Solution: Apple recognized the opportunity to simplify the digital music journey and create a more integrated, user-friendly experience. With the introduction of the iPod and iTunes, Apple significantly reduced the number of steps required for users to find, download, and listen to music:

1. Open iTunes on a computer (pre-installed on Apple devices)
2. Search for a song in the iTunes Store, which offered a vast library of legal, high-quality music.
3. Preview the song directly within iTunes
4. Purchase and download the song with a single click
5. Connect the iPod to the computer, and the song is automatically synced
6. Use the iPod's intuitive click-wheel interface to navigate and play the song easily

By simplifying the music discovery, purchase, and listening process, Apple made it much easier for users to enjoy their favourite music on the go. The iPod's iconic click-wheel interface, which allowed users to access any song within just a few clicks, was a key factor in its ease of use and popularity.

The Impact: Apple's simplification of the digital music journey had a profound impact on the music industry and consumer behaviour:

1. **Legitimizing digital music:** By offering a simple, legal way to purchase digital music, Apple helped combat music piracy and legitimize the digital music market.
2. **Changing music consumption habits:** The iPod and iTunes made it easy for people to carry their entire music library with them, leading to a shift in how people consumed music. Listening to music on the go became more common, and the concept of the personal soundtrack emerged.
3. **Disrupting the music industry:** Apple's business model, which allowed users to purchase individual songs rather than entire albums, disrupted the traditional music industry and forced record labels to adapt to the new digital landscape.
4. **Defining a new product category:** The iPod's success established the portable digital music player as a must-have device and set the standard for future products in the category.
5. **Paving the way for future innovations:** The iPod and iTunes laid the foundation for Apple's future innovations, such as the iPhone and the App Store, which similarly focused on simplifying and integrating complex processes into user-friendly experiences.

Apple's iPod and iTunes demonstrate the power of simplifying customer journeys to create disruptive innovation. By reducing the number of steps required to find, purchase, and listen to digital music, Apple transformed the music industry and changed consumer behaviour.

Nest Thermostat

Nest Labs, a smart home technology company, disrupted the home heating and cooling industry by simplifying the customer journey associated with controlling home temperature through its innovative Nest Learning Thermostat.

Before the Nest Thermostat, the process of controlling home temperature was often complicated and inefficient:

1. Users had to manually adjust their thermostats throughout the day to maintain a comfortable temperature.
2. Programming a thermostat was often a complex and time-consuming process, requiring users to navigate confusing menus and input multiple settings.
3. Many users lacked the knowledge or motivation to optimize their thermostat settings for energy efficiency.
4. Users often forget to adjust their thermostat when leaving home or going to sleep, leading to wasted energy and higher bills.
5. Traditional thermostats provided limited feedback on energy usage, making it difficult for users to understand and optimize their consumption.

These challenges led to a suboptimal user experience and significant energy waste in many homes.

Nest's Solution: Nest Labs recognized the opportunity to simplify the home temperature control journey and create a more user-friendly, energy-efficient solution. The Nest Learning Thermostat introduced several key innovations that reduced the number of steps and complexity involved in managing home temperature:

1. **Auto-scheduling:** The Nest Thermostat automatically learns the user's temperature preferences and creates a personalized schedule, eliminating the need for manual programming
2. **Auto-away:** The thermostat uses motion sensors to detect when the user

is away from home and automatically adjusts the temperature to save energy

3. **Remote control:** Users can easily adjust the temperature from their smartphone or tablet, eliminating the need to physically interact with the thermostat
4. **Energy history:** The Nest Thermostat provides clear, actionable feedback on energy usage, helping users understand and optimize their consumption
5. **Intuitive interface:** The thermostat features a simple, intuitive interface that makes it easy for users to adjust settings and view information at a glance

By simplifying the process of controlling home temperature and providing intelligent, automated features, Nest made it much easier for users to maintain a comfortable, energy-efficient home.

The Impact: The Nest Learning Thermostat's simplification of the home temperature control journey had a significant impact on the industry and consumer behaviour:

1. **Energy savings:** By optimizing temperature settings and reducing waste, the Nest Thermostat helped users save significant amounts of energy and money on their heating and cooling bills.
2. **Increased awareness of energy consumption:** The Nest Thermostat's energy history and feedback features helped raise awareness of energy consumption and encouraged users to adopt more energy-efficient habits.
3. **Disrupting the thermostat industry:** Nest's innovative, user-friendly approach to temperature control disrupted the traditional thermostat industry and forced established players to develop their own smart, connected devices.
4. **Popularizing the smart home:** The Nest Thermostat was one of the first widely-adopted smart home devices, helping to popularize the concept of the connected home and paving the way for future innovations in the

space.

5. **Acquisition by Google:** In 2014, Google acquired Nest Labs for $3.2 billion, validating the company's disruptive potential and setting the stage for further integration of Nest's technology into Google's smart home ecosystem.

The Nest Learning Thermostat is a powerful example of how simplifying customer journeys can lead to disruptive innovation. By reducing the complexity and steps involved in controlling home temperature, Nest created a more user-friendly, energy-efficient solution that transformed the thermostat industry.

In conclusion, simplifying customer journeys and reducing the number of steps required to achieve a goal is a powerful strategy for creating disruptive innovation. By focusing on convenience, efficiency, and ease of use, companies can transform the customer experience, differentiate themselves from competitors, and create entirely new markets. As the examples demonstrate, simplification can be a disruptive force that fundamentally changes the way industries operate and customers behave. For companies seeking to drive innovation and growth, simplifying customer journeys should be a top priority.

* * *

8

Hyper-Personalization

Hyper-personalization is a powerful strategy for creating disruptive innovation by offering highly tailored products, services, or experiences that cater to individual customer preferences and needs. By leveraging data, artificial intelligence (AI), and advanced technologies, companies can deliver personalized solutions that set them apart from competitors and create unparalleled value for their customers.

1. **Data Collection and Analysis:** The foundation of hyper-personalization lies in collecting and analyzing vast amounts of customer data. This data can include demographics, browsing behaviour, purchase history, social media interactions, and more. By gathering and processing this data, companies can gain deep insights into individual customer preferences, needs, and behaviours.
2. **AI and Machine Learning:** Advanced AI and machine learning algorithms play a crucial role in hyper-personalization. These technologies enable companies to process and analyze massive datasets in real-time, identifying patterns, predicting customer behaviour, and generating personalized recommendations. AI-powered systems can continuously learn and adapt based on customer interactions, refining their personalization strategies over time.
3. **Personalized Recommendations:** One of the most common applications

of hyper-personalization is providing personalized product or content recommendations. By analyzing customer data, companies can suggest products, services, or experiences that are highly relevant to each individual. This not only enhances the customer experience but also drives increased engagement, loyalty, and sales.

4. **Customized Products and Services:** Hyper-personalization enables companies to offer customized products and services tailored to individual preferences. This can range from personalized clothing and accessories to customized financial services and insurance plans. By allowing customers to co-create and configure products or services based on their specific needs, companies can differentiate themselves and create stronger emotional connections with their customers.

5. **Personalized Marketing and Communication:** Hyper-personalization extends to marketing and communication strategies as well. By leveraging customer data, companies can deliver highly targeted and personalized marketing messages across various channels, such as email, social media, and mobile apps. Personalized communication can include addressing customers by name, recommending products based on their interests, and providing relevant content and offers at the right time.

6. **Predictive and Proactive Services:** Hyper-personalization enables companies to anticipate customer needs and provide proactive services. By analyzing customer data and behaviour patterns, companies can predict when a customer might need a particular product or service and proactively offer solutions. This level of anticipation and proactive service can create a strong competitive advantage and foster long-term customer loyalty.

7. **Privacy and Data Security:** While hyper-personalization relies on extensive data collection and analysis, companies must prioritize customer privacy and data security. Transparent data practices, secure data storage, and robust privacy policies are essential to maintaining customer trust and complying with regulations such as GDPR and CCPA.

Stitch Fix

Stitch Fix is an innovative company that combines AI-driven algorithms with human expertise to provide hyper-personalized clothing and styling recommendations to its customers. By offering a highly tailored and convenient shopping experience, Stitch Fix has disrupted the traditional retail model and created a new market for personalized fashion services.

1. **Data-Driven Style Profile:** When customers sign up for Stitch Fix, they complete a detailed style profile that captures their preferences, sizes, budgets, and lifestyles. This profile includes questions about preferred colors, patterns, styles, and occasions, as well as body measurements and fit preferences. The rich data collected through these style profiles forms the foundation for Stitch Fix's hyper-personalization engine.

2. **AI-Powered Recommendations:** Stitch Fix employs advanced AI and machine learning algorithms to analyze customer data and generate personalized clothing recommendations. The algorithms take into account various factors, such as style preferences, past feedback, and current fashion trends, to curate a selection of items that are most likely to appeal to each individual customer.

3. **Human Stylists:** While AI powers the initial recommendations, Stitch Fix also leverages the expertise of human stylists to refine and personalize the final selections. Stylists review the AI-generated recommendations, taking into account the customer's style profile, feedback from previous Fixes, and any specific requests or notes. This human touch ensures that each Fix is truly tailored to the individual and adds a level of personalization that goes beyond pure algorithmic recommendations.

4. **Personalized Fixes:** Based on the AI recommendations and stylist input, Stitch Fix sends each customer a personalized "Fix" containing five clothing and accessory items. Customers can try on the items at home, keep what they like, and return what they don't want. Stitch Fix uses the feedback from each Fix to further refine its personalization algorithms, continuously improving the accuracy and relevance of future

recommendations.
5. **Flexible Subscription Model:** Stitch Fix offers a flexible subscription model that allows customers to receive Fixes on a schedule that suits their needs, whether that's every two weeks, monthly, or quarterly. This flexibility, combined with the convenience of home try-on and free returns, has made Stitch Fix an attractive alternative to traditional retail shopping.
6. **Expanded Offerings:** Over time, Stitch Fix has expanded its offerings to include a wider range of sizes, styles, and price points, catering to a diverse customer base. The company has also introduced new services, such as "Stitch Fix Freestyle," which allows customers to shop directly from a personalized online store based on their style profile and past Fixes.

Stitch Fix's hyper-personalized approach has disrupted the traditional retail industry in several ways:

1. **Convenience:** By offering a curated shopping experience that eliminates the need for customers to visit physical stores or browse endless online options, Stitch Fix has made shopping for clothes more convenient and time-efficient.
2. **Personalization at Scale:** Stitch Fix has demonstrated that hyper-personalization can be achieved at scale through the combination of AI and human expertise. This has challenged the notion that personalized services are only viable for niche or luxury markets.
3. **Data-Driven Insights:** The vast amount of data collected by Stitch Fix has enabled the company to gain deep insights into customer preferences and behaviors, allowing them to stay ahead of fashion trends and optimize inventory management.

Stitch Fix's disruptive innovation has not only attracted a loyal customer base but has also inspired other retailers to invest in personalization strategies. By leveraging hyper-personalization, Stitch Fix has created a new market for personalized fashion services and has set a new standard for customer-centric retail experiences.

Spotify

Spotify, a leading music streaming platform, has disrupted the music industry by offering a hyper-personalized listening experience that adapts to each user's unique tastes and preferences.

1. **Taste Profile:** When users sign up for Spotify, the platform begins building a "Taste Profile" based on their listening history, playlists, and interactions with the app. This profile captures users' musical preferences, including favourite artists, genres, and songs. As users continue to listen and engage with the platform, their Taste Profile becomes increasingly refined and accurate.
2. **Personalized Playlists:** One of Spotify's most popular and disruptive features is its personalized playlists. Using AI and machine learning algorithms, Spotify analyzes users' Taste Profiles to create custom playlists tailored to their individual preferences. Playlists like "Discover Weekly," "Daily Mix," and "Release Radar" introduce users to new music and artists based on their listening history and behaviour, ensuring a constantly evolving and personalized music discovery experience.
3. **Contextual Recommendations:** Spotify takes hyper-personalization a step further by considering context and user behaviour when making recommendations. The platform analyzes factors such as time of day, device type, and even user activity (e.g., working out, studying, or relaxing) to suggest playlists and songs that fit the user's current mood and situation. This level of contextual awareness creates a highly engaging and immersive listening experience.
4. **Collaborative Playlists:** Spotify allows users to create and share collaborative playlists with friends, family, or the wider Spotify community. These playlists foster a sense of connection and discovery, as users

can contribute songs and see what others are adding in real time. Collaborative playlists not only enhance the social aspect of music listening but also provide Spotify with valuable data on user connections and shared musical interests.

5. **Data-Driven Artist Insights:** Spotify's hyper-personalization extends beyond the listener experience. The platform provides artists with detailed insights into their audience's demographics, listening habits, and geographic distribution. These insights help artists understand their fan base, inform tour planning, and guide marketing strategies. By empowering artists with data-driven insights, Spotify has disrupted the traditional music industry model and created new opportunities for artist-fan connections.

6. **Podcast Personalization:** In recent years, Spotify has expanded its focus to include podcasts, applying its hyper-personalization capabilities to this growing medium. The platform recommends podcasts based on users' listening history, interests, and the content of their favourite music genres and playlists. This integration of music and podcast personalization has positioned Spotify as a comprehensive audio entertainment platform.

Spotify's hyper-personalized approach has disrupted the music industry in several key ways:

1. **Shift in Music Consumption:** By offering a vast library of music and personalized recommendations, Spotify has changed the way people discover, consume, and engage with music. Users no longer rely on traditional radio or physical albums to find new music; instead, they turn to Spotify's algorithmically curated playlists and personalized suggestions.

2. **Data-Driven Music Industry:** Spotify's data-driven insights have transformed the way artists, labels, and marketers approach the music industry. The platform's ability to track user behaviour and preferences has provided unprecedented visibility into audience engagement, enabling

more targeted and effective marketing and promotional strategies.
3. **Democratization of Music Discovery:** Spotify's hyper-personalization has democratized music discovery by exposing users to a wider range of artists and genres. Independent and emerging artists have gained increased visibility and opportunities to reach new audiences through Spotify's personalized playlists and algorithmic recommendations.

By leveraging hyper-personalization, Spotify has not only disrupted the music industry but also set a new standard for personalized audio entertainment.

In conclusion, hyper-personalization has emerged as a powerful strategy for creating disruptive innovation. By leveraging data, AI, and advanced technologies, companies can offer highly tailored products, services, and experiences that cater to individual customer preferences and needs. As demonstrated by brands like Stitch Fix and Spotify, hyper-personalization can transform industries, create new markets, and set new standards for customer engagement. By embracing hyper-personalization, companies can differentiate themselves, drive customer loyalty, and unlock new opportunities for growth in an increasingly competitive and customer-centric business landscape.

* * *

9

Tracking Emerging Technologies

Apple introduced the computer mouse in the 1980s, revolutionizing the PC industry. However, Doug Engelbart demonstrated it in 1968.

Steve Mann demonstrated Google Glass in 1981. GPS existed as early as 1973 but was widely adopted only after 2000. Microwave technology was developed in the 1930s but commercialized only in the early 1950s.

Disruptive innovation often stems from the application of emerging technologies in novel ways. However, as the examples of the computer mouse, Google Glass, GPS, and microwave technology demonstrate, there can be a significant time lag between the initial development of a technology and its widespread commercialization and adoption. To create disruptive innovation, companies must be proactive in tracking emerging technologies, understanding their potential applications, and experimenting with how they can be used to create new products, services, and business models.

The Importance of Tracking Emerging Technologies

In today's rapidly evolving technological landscape, it's not enough for companies to simply focus on their existing products and markets. To stay ahead of the curve and create disruptive innovation, companies must have a deep understanding of the emerging technologies that have the potential to transform their industries in the coming years.

As John Kolko notes, "Anything that will be a billion-dollar industry in 10 years is already 10 years old." This means that the technologies that will drive the next wave of disruptive innovation are likely already in existence, even if they are not yet widely known or understood. By tracking these emerging technologies early on, companies can gain a significant competitive advantage and position themselves to create truly disruptive innovations.

Strategies for Tracking Emerging Technologies

Read Tech Journals and Publications: One of the most effective ways to stay up-to-date on emerging technologies is to regularly read tech journals and publications. These sources provide in-depth coverage of the latest technological developments, trends, and breakthroughs across a wide range of fields, from artificial intelligence and blockchain to biotechnology and materials science.

Some key tech journals and publications to follow include:

- MIT Technology Review
- Wired
- IEEE Spectrum
- Nature
- Science
- Harvard Business Review

By dedicating time each week to reading these sources, companies can gain a comprehensive understanding of the emerging technologies that are shaping their industries and identify potential opportunities for disruptive innovation.

Attend Tech Conferences and Events: Another important strategy for tracking emerging technologies is to attend tech conferences and events. These gatherings bring together leading researchers, entrepreneurs, and innovators to share their latest work and insights, providing a unique opportunity to learn about cutting-edge technologies and their potential applications.

Some notable tech conferences and events include:

- CES (Consumer Electronics Show)
- SXSW (South by Southwest)
- TED (Technology, Entertainment, Design)
- Web Summit
- MIT EmTech (Emerging Technologies)
- Singularity University Global Summit

By attending these events and engaging with the latest technological developments and ideas, companies can gain valuable exposure to emerging technologies and build relationships with key players in the tech industry.

Collaborate with Academic Institutions and Research Labs: Academic institutions and research labs are often at the forefront of technological innovation, conducting cutting-edge research and development that can lead to disruptive breakthroughs. By collaborating with these organizations, companies can gain early access to emerging technologies and work together to explore their potential commercial applications.

Collaboration can take many forms, from sponsored research projects and joint ventures to technology licensing and talent recruitment. By building strong relationships with academic institutions and research labs, companies can tap into a rich source of technological innovation and expertise.

Foster a Culture of Curiosity and Experimentation: To effectively track and leverage emerging technologies, companies must foster a culture of curiosity and experimentation. This means encouraging employees to stay up-to-date on the latest technological developments, providing resources and support for learning and skills development, and creating opportunities for hands-on experimentation and prototyping.

Some ways to foster a culture of curiosity and experimentation include:

- Hosting internal tech talks and workshops
- Providing access to online learning platforms and courses
- Encouraging participation in hackathons and innovation challenges
- Allocating time and resources for side projects and exploratory work
- Celebrating and rewarding innovative ideas and initiatives

By creating an environment that values and supports technological exploration and experimentation, companies can better position themselves to identify and capitalize on emerging technologies for disruptive innovation.

Leveraging Emerging Technologies for Disruptive Innovation

Tracking emerging technologies is just the first step in creating disruptive innovation. To truly leverage these technologies for business impact, companies must be proactive in exploring their potential applications and experimenting with how they can be used to create new products, services, and business models.

Some key steps in this process include:

1. **Identify Relevant Technologies:** Not all emerging technologies will be relevant or applicable to a given company or industry. The first step in leveraging emerging technologies for disruptive innovation is to identify which technologies are most likely to impact your business in the coming years. This requires a deep understanding of your industry, customers, and competitive landscape, as well as a broad perspective on

technological trends and developments.

2. **Understand Potential Applications:** Once you've identified relevant technologies, the next step is to understand their potential applications and use cases. This may involve conducting market research, talking to customers and industry experts, and brainstorming with cross-functional teams to explore how these technologies could be used to solve existing problems or create new opportunities.

3. **Experiment and Prototype:** To truly understand the potential of an emerging technology, it's important to move beyond theoretical discussions and into hands-on experimentation and prototyping. This may involve building minimum viable products (MVPs), conducting pilot tests with customers, or partnering with technology providers to explore proof-of-concept applications.

4. **Iterate and Refine:** Disruptive innovation rarely happens overnight. It often requires a process of iterative experimentation, learning, and refinement to fully realize the potential of an emerging technology. As you experiment and prototype with new technologies, be prepared to pivot and adapt based on feedback and insights from customers, partners, and internal stakeholders.

5. **Scale and Commercialize:** Once you've validated the potential of an emerging technology and developed a compelling application or use case, the final step is to scale and commercialize your innovation. This may involve integrating the technology into existing products and services, launching new offerings, or even creating entirely new business models and revenue streams.

Apple and the iPhone

The introduction of the iPhone in 2007 is a prime example of how Apple leveraged emerging technologies to create a disruptive innovation that transformed the mobile phone industry.

Prior to the iPhone, the mobile phone market was dominated by devices with limited functionality and clunky user interfaces. Smartphones, such as BlackBerry and Palm Treo, were primarily used by business professionals for email and basic web browsing. Consumer-oriented mobile phones were mainly used for calling and text messaging, with limited multimedia capabilities.

Apple, known for its innovative products like the iPod and iMac, saw an opportunity to revolutionize the mobile phone market by creating a device that combined the functionality of a smartphone with the ease of use and design appeal of a consumer device.

Tracking and Leveraging Emerging Technologies: To create the iPhone, Apple tracked and leveraged several emerging technologies:

1. **Multi-touch Screens:** Apple was one of the first companies to recognize the potential of multi-touch screens for mobile devices. By using a capacitive touchscreen that could detect multiple touch points simultaneously, Apple was able to create a highly responsive and intuitive user interface that allowed users to interact with their devices using natural gestures like tapping, swiping, and pinching.
2. **Motion Sensors:** Apple incorporated motion sensors, such as accelerometers and gyroscopes, into the iPhone, enabling features like automatic screen rotation and motion-based gaming. These sensors also laid the foundation for future innovations in mobile computing, such as fitness tracking and augmented reality applications.
3. **Mobile Internet Connectivity:** The iPhone was one of the first mobile devices to offer a full-featured web browser that could display web pages in their entirety. By leveraging advances in mobile internet connectivity, such as 3G networks and Wi-Fi, Apple was able to create a device that could access the internet from virtually anywhere, transforming the way people consumed information and media on the go.
4. **App-based Software Architecture:** Perhaps the most significant technological innovation of the iPhone was its app-based software architecture. By creating an ecosystem of third-party developers who could build and

distribute apps through the App Store, Apple was able to tap into a vast pool of creativity and innovation, leading to an explosion of new use cases and functionalities for mobile devices.

The combination of these emerging technologies, along with Apple's signature design and user experience, created a device that was truly disruptive to the mobile phone industry.

The iPhone's touchscreen interface and intuitive navigation made it accessible to a wide range of consumers, not just business users. Its ability to access the full internet and run third-party apps transformed the mobile phone from a communication device into a versatile computing platform.

The launch of the App Store in 2008 further accelerated the iPhone's disruptive impact, creating a new economy of mobile software and services. Developers flocked to the platform, creating a wide range of innovative apps that leveraged the iPhone's unique capabilities, from mobile gaming and social networking to productivity and e-commerce.

As a result of the iPhone's success, other mobile phone manufacturers were forced to adapt and innovate, leading to a rapid evolution of smartphone technology and the emergence of new platforms like Android. The iPhone also paved the way for future innovations in mobile computing, such as tablets, wearables, and the Internet of Things.

Tesla

Tesla, founded in 2003, has leveraged emerging technologies to disrupt the automotive industry and accelerate the adoption of electric vehicles (EVs) worldwide.

Before Tesla, the electric vehicle market was dominated by small, niche players producing low-range, low-performance vehicles. The prevailing opinion in the automotive industry was that EVs were impractical and unsuitable for mass-market adoption due to limitations in battery technology, charging infrastructure, and consumer preferences.

Tesla, led by entrepreneur Elon Musk, set out to challenge these assumptions and create a new paradigm for electric vehicles.

Tracking and Leveraging Emerging Technologies: To create its disruptive electric vehicles, Tesla tracked and leveraged several emerging technologies:

1. **Lithium-Ion Battery Technology:** Tesla recognized the potential of lithium-ion batteries, which were primarily used in consumer electronics, to power electric vehicles. By investing heavily in battery research and development, Tesla was able to create high-performance battery packs that could deliver long ranges and fast charging times, overcoming one of the main barriers to EV adoption.
2. **Electric Powertrain Technology:** Tesla developed advanced electric powertrain technology, including high-efficiency motors and power electronics, that could deliver instant torque and superior performance compared to internal combustion engines. This allowed Tesla to create EVs that were not only environmentally friendly but also fun and exciting to drive.
3. **Autonomous Driving Technology:** Tesla has been at the forefront of autonomous driving technology, leveraging advances in sensors, computer vision, and machine learning to create increasingly sophisticated Autopilot systems. While fully self-driving cars are still in development, Tesla's progress in this area has positioned the company as a leader in the future of transportation.
4. **Over-the-Air Software Updates:** Tesla pioneered the use of over-the-air software updates in the automotive industry, allowing the company to continuously improve and add new features to its vehicles even after they have been sold. This has created a new paradigm for the automotive industry, where cars can get better over time and adapt to changing customer needs and preferences.

Tesla's combination of these emerging technologies, along with its focus on design and performance, has created a new class of electric vehicles that are disrupting the traditional automotive industry.

Tesla's vehicles, such as the Model S, Model X, and Model 3, have demonstrated that EVs can offer compelling performance, style, and functionality, challenging the notion that electric cars are inferior to gasoline-powered vehicles. The company's success has forced traditional automakers to invest heavily in EV development, accelerating the transition to a more sustainable transportation future.

In addition to its technological innovations, Tesla has also disrupted the automotive sales and service model. By selling directly to consumers and providing over-the-air updates, Tesla has created a more streamlined and customer-centric experience that challenges the traditional dealership model.

To conclude, tracking emerging technologies is a critical strategy for companies seeking to create disruptive innovation. By staying up-to-date on the latest technological developments, attending conferences and events, collaborating with academic institutions and research labs, and fostering a culture of curiosity and experimentation, companies can position themselves to identify and leverage emerging technologies for business impact.

However, tracking emerging technologies is just the first step. To truly create disruptive innovation, companies must be proactive in exploring the potential applications of these technologies, experimenting with new ideas and approaches, and iterating and refining their innovations based on feedback and insights from customers and stakeholders.

* * *

10

Tracking Emerging Competitors

In today's rapidly evolving business landscape, staying ahead of the curve requires more than just keeping an eye on established competitors. To create truly disruptive innovations, companies must also track and learn from emerging competitors who are bringing new ideas, technologies, and business models to the market. By identifying these emerging threats and opportunities early on, and by strategically leveraging the insights gained from them, companies can position themselves to lead the way in driving industry transformation and staying ahead of the competition.

Identifying Emerging Competitors: The first step in tracking emerging competitors is to identify them. This requires a proactive approach to monitoring industry trends, attending relevant events, and analyzing market shifts. Pay close attention to venture capital investments and funding rounds, as these can provide valuable insights into which startups are gaining traction and potentially disrupting the market. Regularly review the offerings and value propositions of new entrants to assess their potential impact on your industry.

Assessing the Disruptive Potential of Emerging Competitors: Once you have identified emerging competitors, it is crucial to assess their disruptive potential. Evaluate their unique value propositions and determine how they differentiate themselves from established players in the market. Analyze their target market and customer segments to understand if they are addressing unmet needs or targeting underserved markets. Consider their scalability and growth potential, as well as their pricing strategies and business models, to gauge their long-term viability and potential impact on your industry.

Learning from Emerging Competitors: Tracking emerging competitors is not just about staying informed; it is also an opportunity to learn from their innovative approaches and strategies. Study how they are disrupting the market and identify gaps in your own offerings or business model. Use these insights to adapt and improve your products, services, and processes. Foster a culture of continuous learning and innovation within your organization to stay agile and responsive to emerging threats and opportunities.

Collaborating with or Acquiring Emerging Competitors: In some cases, it may be beneficial to collaborate with or acquire emerging competitors to enhance your own disruptive potential. Explore potential partnerships or collaborations that can help you expand your capabilities, enter new markets, or accelerate innovation. Consider strategic investments or acquisitions to integrate complementary technologies or expertise into your organization. By leveraging synergies with emerging competitors, you can position your company to lead the way in disruptive innovation.

Embracing Disruption as an Ongoing Process: Finally, it is essential to recognize that creating disruptive innovation is an ongoing process. Continuously monitor and assess the competitive landscape to identify new threats and opportunities. Encourage experimentation and risk-taking within your organization to foster a culture of innovation. Invest in research and development to stay at the forefront of technological advancements and market trends. By cultivating a disruptive mindset throughout your organization, you can position your company to not only withstand disruption but also to lead the charge in driving industry transformation.

Netflix & Blockbuster

In the late 1990s and early 2000s, Blockbuster was the dominant player in the video rental industry, with a vast network of brick-and-mortar stores. However, the company failed to recognize the disruptive potential of DVD-by-mail and streaming services, which were pioneered by Netflix.

Netflix, founded by Reed Hastings and Marc Randolph, began as a DVD-by-mail rental service, offering a more convenient alternative to traditional video rental stores. Despite this emerging threat, Blockbuster remained focused on its brick-and-mortar model, which relied heavily on late fees for revenue.

As Netflix's DVD-by-mail service grew in popularity, Blockbuster attempted to launch its own online rental service. However, the company was slow to invest in the necessary technology and infrastructure, and its online offering was inferior to Netflix in terms of selection and user experience. Blockbuster failed to learn from Netflix's success and adapt its business model accordingly.

In the meantime, Netflix's founders keenly observed the emergence of streaming technology to disrupt the entertainment industry further. As internet speeds improved and streaming technology advanced, Netflix closely monitored the activities of emerging competitors such as YouTube and Hulu. They recognized the growing demand for online video content and the potential for streaming to revolutionize the way people consume entertainment.

In 2007, Netflix introduced its streaming service, which allowed subscribers to watch movies and TV shows online. This move marked the beginning of their transition into a streaming-focused company. Blockbuster, on the other hand, failed to anticipate the shift toward streaming video and was slow to react to this new threat.

Over the next few years, Netflix continued to track and analyze the strategies of emerging competitors in the streaming space. They invested heavily in developing their own proprietary technology and building a robust library of licensed content. In 2013, Netflix took a bold step by launching its first original series, "House of Cards," which was a massive success and demonstrated the potential for original content in the streaming era.

By closely monitoring emerging competitors and anticipating shifts in consumer behaviour, Netflix was able to pivot its business model and disrupt the entertainment industry not once but twice. They transformed from a DVD-by-mail service to a global streaming giant.

Despite belated attempts to adapt, such as eliminating late fees and introducing a streaming service, Blockbuster was unable to catch up to Netflix. The company filed for bankruptcy in 2010 and has since largely disappeared, with only a handful of franchise locations remaining.

The contrasting examples of Blockbuster and Netflix illustrate the importance of tracking emerging competitors, learning from their successes, and leveraging those insights to drive disruptive innovation. While Blockbuster remained tied to its traditional business model and failed to invest in new technologies and consumer trends, Netflix continuously monitored the competitive landscape, adapted its strategies, and disrupted the entertainment industry multiple times. As a result, Netflix has become a leader in the streaming industry, while Blockbuster has become a cautionary tale of the dangers of failing to innovate in the face of disruptive threats.

Barnes & Noble and Amazon

In the mid-1990s, Barnes & Noble was the largest bookseller in the United States, with a vast network of brick-and-mortar stores. However, the company failed to recognize the disruptive potential of online bookselling and e-books, which were pioneered by Amazon.

Amazon, founded by Jeff Bezos in 1994, began as an online bookstore, offering a wider selection of books than traditional retail stores and the convenience of home delivery. Despite this emerging threat, Barnes & Noble remained focused on its physical store model, believing that customers would always prefer to browse and purchase books in person.

As Amazon's online bookstore grew in popularity, Barnes & Noble was slow to adapt and invest in its own online presence. When the company finally launched its online store, barnesandnoble.com, in 1997, it was already playing catch-up to Amazon. Barnes & Noble failed to learn from Amazon's success and leverage the potential of online bookselling.

In the early 2000s, Jeff Bezos noticed that several startups were venturing into the e-book reader device market, but these early attempts were plagued with problems. Despite the issues, Bezos recognized the potential value in the device and believed that it could disrupt the traditional publishing industry.

As technology advanced and e-readers became more affordable, Amazon closely monitored the market and invested in developing its own e-reader. In 2007, Amazon launched the Kindle, which, coupled with the company's vast selection of e-books, revolutionized the way people read and purchased books.

On the other hand, Barnes & Noble was slow to recognize the potential of e-books and e-readers. It wasn't until 2009, two years after the Kindle's launch, that the company introduced its own e-reader, the Nook. Despite heavily investing in the Nook, Barnes & Noble struggled to gain significant market share in the e-reader market, which was already dominated by Amazon.

Over the years, Amazon continued to innovate and expand its offerings, moving beyond books to become a one-stop-shop for a wide range of products and services. The company leveraged its vast customer data to offer personalized recommendations, introduced a loyalty program (Amazon Prime), and invested in new technologies such as AI and cloud computing.

By closely monitoring emerging trends and anticipating shifts in consumer behavior, Amazon was able to continuously disrupt the retail industry and become a global e-commerce giant. In contrast, Barnes & Noble failed to learn from Amazon's success and adapt its business model accordingly. As a result, the company has struggled to compete with Amazon and has seen its market share and profits decline steadily over the years.

In conclusion, tracking emerging competitors is a critical strategy for creating disruptive innovation. By identifying potential disruptors, assessing their impact, learning from their approaches, and potentially collaborating with or acquiring them, companies can stay ahead of the curve and maintain a competitive edge in an ever-changing business landscape. Embracing disruption as an ongoing process and fostering a culture of innovation is key to long-term success in today's dynamic market environment.

* * *

11

Reimagining Business Models

Disruptive innovation is not just about creating new products or services; it's also about fundamentally rethinking the way businesses operate and create value for customers. One of the most powerful strategies for creating disruptive innovation is to reimagine the business model itself. By challenging traditional assumptions and approaches, companies can unlock new sources of growth and competitive advantage, even in mature or highly commoditized industries.

What is a Business Model?

A business model describes how a company creates, delivers, and captures value. It encompasses the key activities, resources, partnerships, and revenue streams that enable a company to serve its customers and generate profits. Some of the key elements of a business model include:

1. **Value Proposition:** The unique benefits and experiences that a company offers to its customers.
2. **Customer Segments:** The specific groups of customers that a company targets with its products or services.
3. **Channels:** The ways in which a company reaches and interacts with its

customers, such as through retail stores, online platforms, or direct sales.
4. **Revenue Streams:** The ways in which a company generates income, such as through product sales, subscriptions, or advertising.
5. **Key Activities:** The core processes and tasks that a company performs to create and deliver value to customers.
6. **Key Resources:** The assets and capabilities that a company relies on to execute its business model, such as technology, intellectual property, or human capital.
7. **Key Partnerships:** The external relationships and collaborations that a company leverages to enhance its value creation and delivery.
8. **Cost Structure:** The key costs and expenses that a company incurs in operating its business model.

Why Reimagine Business Models?

In many industries, traditional business models have remained largely unchanged for decades, even as new technologies and customer preferences have emerged. This creates an opportunity for disruptive innovation by companies that are willing to fundamentally rethink their business models and challenge industry conventions.

Reimagining the business model can enable companies to:

1. **Create new sources of value:** By rethinking the way they create and deliver value to customers, companies can tap into new sources of differentiation and competitive advantage.
2. **Reach new customer segments:** Innovative business models can enable companies to serve customer segments that were previously unprofitable or inaccessible, such as low-income consumers or niche markets.
3. **Disrupt industry economics:** By fundamentally changing the cost structure or revenue streams of an industry, disruptive business models can create a new basis for competition and render traditional approaches

obsolete.
4. **Adapt to changing technologies and customer needs:** As new technologies emerge and customer preferences evolve, reimagining the business model can help companies stay ahead of the curve and remain relevant in a changing market.

Strategies for Reimagining Business Models

a) Identify Industry Assumptions and Orthodoxies: The first step in reimagining a business model is to identify the underlying assumptions and orthodoxies that shape the way an industry operates. These may include assumptions about customer needs and preferences, pricing and revenue models, or the roles and relationships of different industry players.

By systematically challenging these assumptions and asking "what if" questions, companies can begin to identify opportunities for business model innovation. For example:

- What if we offered our product as a subscription service instead of a one-time purchase?
- What if we partnered with a complementary service provider to create a bundled offering?
- What if we used technology to automate key processes and reduce costs?

b) Embrace New Technologies and Platforms: Advances in digital technology and platforms are creating new opportunities for business model innovation across industries. By leveraging these technologies, companies can create new value propositions, reach new customers, and disrupt traditional industry economics.

Some examples of technology-enabled business model innovations include:

- Platform-based business models that connect buyers and sellers, such as

Airbnb or Uber
- Subscription-based models that provide ongoing access to products or services, such as Netflix or Spotify
- Freemium models that offer a basic service for free and charge for premium features, such as Dropbox or LinkedIn
- Pay-per-use models that charge based on consumption, such as cloud computing or shared mobility services

c) Redefine the Value Proposition: Another key strategy for business model innovation is to fundamentally redefine the value proposition offered to customers. This may involve shifting from a product-based to a service-based model, or from a transactional to a relationship-based approach.

Some examples of value proposition innovations include:

- **Servitization:** Offering products as a service, such as Rolls-Royce's "Power by the Hour" model for jet engines
- **Customization:** Offering highly personalized products or experiences, such as Stitch Fix's curated clothing boxes
- **Convenience:** Offering time-saving or hassle-free solutions, such as Amazon's one-click ordering or Instacart's grocery delivery service
- **Sustainability:** Offering environmentally friendly or socially responsible products and services, such as Patagonia's recycled clothing or TOMS' one-for-one giving model

d) Collaborate and Co-Create: with Ecosystem Partners In today's interconnected business environment, companies rarely succeed in isolation. Reimagining the business model often involves collaborating and co-creating with a broader ecosystem of partners, including suppliers, distributors, technology providers, and even competitors.

By leveraging the capabilities and resources of ecosystem partners, companies can create new sources of value and innovation that would be difficult to achieve on their own. Some examples of ecosystem-based business model innovations include:

- **Platform ecosystems:** Building a platform that enables third-party developers and partners to create complementary products and services, such as Apple's App Store or Amazon's Marketplace
- **Co-branding and bundling:** Partnering with complementary brands to create integrated offerings, such as Nike and Apple's co-branded smartwatch
- **Open innovation:** Collaborating with external partners to jointly develop new products or services, such as Procter & Gamble's Connect + Develop program

e) **Experiment and Iterate:** Reimagining a business model is rarely a one-time event. It often involves ongoing experimentation, learning, and iteration to find the right approach that creates value for customers and the business.

Companies can use a variety of approaches to experiment with new business models, such as:

- **Pilot programs:** Testing new business models with a small group of customers or in a specific market before scaling up
- **Spin-offs and subsidiaries:** Creating separate business units or entities to incubate and grow new business models
- **Partnerships and joint ventures:** Collaborating with external partners to test and validate new business models
- **Acquisitions:** Buying and integrating companies with complementary business models or capabilities

By embracing a culture of experimentation and learning, companies can continuously evolve and adapt their business models in response to changing market conditions and customer needs.

Hilti

Hilti, a Liechtenstein-based manufacturer of high-quality power tools and equipment for the construction industry, has successfully reimagined its business model to create disruptive innovation in a highly competitive and commoditized market.

Traditionally, Hilti operated on a straightforward product sales model. The company designed and manufactured premium power tools, which it sold to construction companies through a network of distributors and retailers. While Hilti's products were known for their quality and reliability, the company faced intense competition from lower-priced rivals and struggled to differentiate itself in a market increasingly driven by price.

In the early 2000s, Hilti recognized that its traditional business model was no longer sustainable in the face of changing customer needs and market conditions. The company set out to reimagine its business model to create new sources of value and differentiation.

Reimagining the Business Model: Hilti's journey to business model innovation began with a deep understanding of its customers' needs and pain points. Through extensive research and engagement with construction companies, Hilti realized that its customers were not just looking for high-quality tools, but also for ways to manage their tools more efficiently and effectively.

Construction companies often struggled with the cost and complexity of managing large fleets of tools across multiple job sites. They had to deal with issues such as tool maintenance, repair, and replacement, as well as inventory tracking and compliance with safety regulations. These challenges distracted them from their core business of construction and eroded their productivity and profitability.

Based on these insights, Hilti reimagined its business model to offer a comprehensive tool management service to construction companies. Instead of simply selling tools, Hilti would provide its customers with ongoing access to a full range of tools and equipment, as well as value-added services such as maintenance, repair, and fleet management.

The new business model, called Hilti Fleet Management, worked as follows:

1. Customers would sign up for a subscription-based service that gave them access to a customized fleet of Hilti tools and equipment, tailored to their specific needs and job requirements.
2. Hilti would deliver the tools to the customer's job site and provide ongoing maintenance, repair, and replacement services to ensure optimal performance and reliability.
3. Customers would pay a monthly fee based on the size and composition of their tool fleet, as well as the level of service they required.
4. Hilti would use advanced technologies such as RFID tracking and data analytics to help customers optimize their tool usage, reduce costs, and improve productivity.

By shifting from a transactional product sales model to a subscription-based service model, Hilti was able to create a new source of recurring revenue and differentiate itself in a highly commoditized market. Customers benefited from reduced tool ownership costs, improved tool availability and reliability, and greater flexibility to scale their tool fleet up or down based on changing project needs.

Results and Impact: Hilti's business model innovation has been a resounding success. Since launching Hilti Fleet Management in 2001, the company has seen steady growth in its service business, with more than 1 million tools under management and over 100,000 customers worldwide.

The service model has also helped Hilti to differentiate itself from competitors and build stronger, more loyal customer relationships. By providing ongoing value and support beyond the initial product sale, Hilti has been able to position itself as a trusted partner to construction companies, helping them to improve their operational efficiency and productivity.

Hilti's success has inspired other companies in the construction industry and beyond to rethink their own business models and explore new ways to create value for customers.

Rolls-Royce

Rolls-Royce, a British multinational engineering company known for its high-performance aircraft engines, has successfully reimagined its business model to create disruptive innovation in the aviation industry.

Traditionally, Rolls-Royce's business model revolved around the sale of aircraft engines to airlines and aircraft manufacturers. The company would design, manufacture, and sell engines and then provide maintenance and repair services on a time and materials basis. This model was highly dependent on the volume of engine sales and left Rolls-Royce exposed to the cyclical nature of the aviation industry.

In the 1960s, Rolls-Royce began to experience significant challenges with its business model. The development of new, more complex engines required significant upfront investment, while the cost of maintenance and repair was increasing. At the same time, airlines were looking for ways to reduce their operating costs and improve the predictability of their expenses.

Reimagining the Business Model: To address these challenges, Rolls-Royce began to reimagine its business model. The company recognized that its customers were not just buying engines, but rather the power and performance that those engines delivered. This insight led Rolls-Royce to develop a new business model called "Power by the Hour."

Under the Power by the Hour model, Rolls-Royce would no longer sell engines outright to its customers. Instead, it would provide airlines with a comprehensive engine maintenance and support service, charging them based on the number of hours flown by the engines.

The Power by the Hour model worked as follows:

1. Airlines would pay Rolls-Royce a fixed hourly rate for each engine in service, based on the number of hours flown.
2. Rolls-Royce would assume responsibility for the maintenance, repair, and overhaul of the engines, ensuring their optimal performance and reliability.
3. Rolls-Royce would use advanced data analytics and predictive main-

tenance techniques to monitor engine performance in real-time and schedule maintenance proactively, minimizing disruption to airline operations.
4. Airlines would benefit from reduced operating costs, improved engine reliability, and greater predictability of expenses, while Rolls-Royce would benefit from a stable, recurring revenue stream.

By shifting from a product-based to a service-based model, Rolls-Royce was able to create a new source of value for its customers and differentiate itself in a highly competitive market. The Power by the Hour model aligned Rolls-Royce's interests with those of its customers, incentivizing the company to maximize engine performance and minimize downtime.

Results and Impact: The Power by the Hour model has been a major success for Rolls-Royce. Since its introduction in the 1960s, the model has evolved and expanded to encompass a wide range of services, from fuel management and flight planning to predictive maintenance and inventory optimization.

Today, Rolls-Royce's service business accounts for more than 50% of its total revenue, with over 80% of its new engine sales covered by Power by the Hour contracts. The model has helped Rolls-Royce to build long-term, strategic relationships with its customers and to differentiate itself from competitors who continue to rely on traditional product sales models.

Spotify—Changing the Revenue Stream and Channels

Spotify, the Swedish audio streaming platform, has revolutionized the music industry by changing the traditional music business model's revenue stream and channel components.

Traditionally, the music industry relied on the sale of physical albums and digital downloads as the primary revenue streams. Spotify disrupted this model by introducing a subscription-based streaming service, where users pay a monthly fee for access to a vast library of music. This shift in the revenue stream allowed Spotify to provide a more affordable and convenient way for consumers to access music, while also providing a recurring revenue stream for the company.

In addition to changing the revenue stream, Spotify also transformed the channels through which music is delivered. Instead of relying on physical distribution or digital downloads, Spotify leveraged the internet and mobile apps to stream music directly to users' devices. This change in the distribution channel made music more accessible and convenient for consumers, allowing them to listen to their favorite songs anytime, anywhere.

By changing the revenue stream and channels, Spotify has not only disrupted the music industry but also paved the way for other streaming services across various media, such as video and podcasts.

Zara—Transforming Key Activities and Partnerships

Zara, the Spanish fast-fashion retailer, has disrupted the traditional fashion industry by transforming its key activities and partnerships.

Traditionally, fashion retailers followed a seasonal model, where designs were created months in advance and manufactured in large batches. Zara disrupted this model by adopting a just-in-time (JIT) manufacturing approach, enabled by a unique combination of key activities and partnerships.

Zara's key activities involve a highly responsive and agile design and production process. The company closely monitors customer preferences and trends, using real-time data to inform its design decisions. New designs are created and produced in small batches, allowing Zara to quickly respond to changing customer demands and minimize the risk of unsold inventory.

To support this agile production process, Zara has transformed its key partnerships. The company has developed a network of local suppliers and manufacturers, enabling it to produce and distribute new designs quickly and efficiently. By fostering close collaborations with its partners, Zara has created a highly responsive and flexible supply chain that can adapt to changing market conditions.

The combination of Zara's transformed key activities and partnerships has allowed the company to disrupt the fashion industry by offering trendy, affordable clothing with unprecedented speed and efficiency. This business model innovation has been widely imitated by other fast-fashion retailers, demonstrating its disruptive impact on the industry.

Coursera—Transforming Key Resources and Customer Segments

Coursera, the online learning platform, has disrupted the traditional education industry by transforming its key resources and customer segments.

Traditionally, higher education relied on physical resources, such as classrooms, textbooks, and faculty, to deliver educational content to students. Coursera disrupted this model by leveraging digital resources, such as online video lectures, interactive assignments, and peer-to-peer learning forums, to deliver educational content remotely. By digitizing its key resources, Coursera has made high-quality education more accessible and affordable to students worldwide.

In addition to transforming its key resources, Coursera has also expanded its customer segments. While traditional higher education primarily targeted students seeking full-time, on-campus degrees, Coursera has focused on serving a broader range of learners, including working professionals, lifelong learners, and students in underserved regions. By offering a wide variety of courses and flexible learning options, Coursera has opened up education to new customer segments that were previously underserved by traditional institutions.

The combination of Coursera's transformed key resources and expanded customer segments has allowed the company to disrupt the education industry and democratize access to high-quality learning opportunities.

Peloton — Changing the Value Proposition and Channels

Peloton, the connected fitness company, has disrupted the traditional fitness industry by changing its value proposition and channels.

Traditionally, the fitness industry revolved around gym memberships and in-person classes. Peloton disrupted this model by offering a unique value proposition: high-quality, interactive fitness experiences that can be accessed from the comfort of one's home. By combining exercise equipment (such as stationary bikes and treadmills) with live and on-demand streaming classes, Peloton has created a new category of connected fitness that offers the motivation and engagement of in-person classes with the convenience and flexibility of at-home workouts.

To deliver this value proposition, Peloton has also transformed its channels. Instead of relying on physical gym locations, Peloton has leveraged digital channels, such as its mobile app and streaming platform, to reach customers directly. This direct-to-consumer approach has allowed Peloton to build strong relationships with its customers and gather valuable data on their preferences and behaviors.

The combination of Peloton's unique value proposition and digital channels has allowed the company to disrupt the fitness industry and create a new market for connected fitness experiences.

These examples demonstrate how disrupting different components of a business model, such as revenue streams, channels, key activities, and partnerships, can lead to disruptive innovation in various industries.

To conclude, reimagining the business model is a powerful strategy for creating disruptive innovation and unlocking new sources of growth and competitive advantage. By challenging traditional industry assumptions, embracing new technologies and platforms, redefining the value proposition, collaborating with ecosystem partners, and experimenting and iterating, companies can fundamentally transform the way they create and capture value.

As the examples demonstrate, business model innovation can take many forms and significantly impact various industries. By embracing a holistic and customer-centric approach to business model design, and continuously adapting and evolving in response to changing market conditions, companies can position themselves for long-term success in an increasingly dynamic and competitive business environment.

* * *

12

Convergence of Industries

In today's rapidly evolving business landscape, the boundaries between industries are becoming increasingly blurred. Companies are recognizing the potential for disruptive innovation by combining elements from different sectors to create novel products, services, and experiences. This chapter explores the concept of industry convergence as a powerful strategy for driving disruptive innovation and examines how companies can leverage this approach to create new market opportunities and stay ahead of the competition.

Understanding Industry Convergence

Industry convergence occurs when two or more distinct industries begin to merge or overlap, creating new market opportunities and disrupting traditional business models. This phenomenon is often driven by technological advancements, changing consumer preferences, and the increasing interconnectedness of the global economy.

Convergence can take many forms, such as:

1. **Technological convergence:** When different technologies are combined to create new products or services, such as the integration of mobile

phones, cameras, and internet connectivity in smartphones.

2. **Market convergence:** When companies from different industries compete in the same market space, such as the convergence of entertainment, telecommunications, and technology companies in the streaming media market.

3. **Functional convergence:** When products or services from different industries are combined to create new offerings that address a specific customer need, such as the convergence of fitness, healthcare, and wearable technology in the wellness industry.

By understanding the various forms of industry convergence, companies can identify opportunities to create disruptive innovations that leverage the strengths of multiple sectors.

Benefits of Industry Convergence

Industry convergence offers several key benefits for companies seeking to create disruptive innovation:

1. **Access to new markets:** By combining elements from different industries, companies can tap into new customer segments and market opportunities that may have been previously inaccessible.

2. **Synergistic value creation:** Convergence allows companies to leverage the strengths and capabilities of multiple industries to create new value propositions that are greater than the sum of their parts.

3. **Differentiation and competitive advantage:** By creating unique and innovative offerings that span multiple industries, companies can differentiate themselves from competitors and establish a sustainable competitive advantage.

4. **Accelerated innovation:** Convergence can foster a culture of cross-disciplinary collaboration and knowledge-sharing, leading to accelerated innovation and the development of breakthrough ideas.

Strategies for Leveraging Industry Convergence

To successfully leverage industry convergence for disruptive innovation, companies should consider the following strategies:

1. **Identify convergence opportunities:** Conduct a thorough analysis of market trends, technological advancements, and customer needs to identify potential areas of convergence between different industries.
2. **Foster cross-functional collaboration:** Encourage collaboration and knowledge-sharing among teams from different disciplines and industries to facilitate the development of novel ideas and solutions.
3. **Develop strategic partnerships:** Form strategic alliances and partnerships with companies from complementary industries to access new technologies, expertise, and market opportunities.
4. **Embrace agility and experimentation:** Adopt an agile and experimental approach to innovation, allowing for rapid prototyping, testing, and iteration of convergent solutions.
5. **Invest in continuous learning:** Foster a culture of continuous learning and encourage employees to stay up-to-date with the latest trends and developments across multiple industries.

Starbucks

Convergence: Coffee + Hospitality + Retail

Starbucks, a global coffee giant, has revolutionized the coffee industry by leveraging the convergence of coffee, hospitality, and retail. What started as a single coffee shop in Seattle's Pike Place Market in 1971 has grown into a global brand with more than 30,000 stores in 80 countries. Starbucks' success can be attributed to its ability to create a unique and compelling customer experience that goes beyond just selling coffee.

Convergence Strategy: Starbucks' convergence strategy is centered on the integration of high-quality coffee, exceptional customer service, and a welcoming retail environment. By combining elements from these different industries, Starbucks has been able to differentiate itself from competitors and create a loyal customer base.

At the core of Starbucks' convergence strategy is its focus on creating a "third place" experience. The company recognizes that people need a place to gather outside of their homes and workplaces, and it has designed its stores to provide a welcoming and comfortable environment that encourages customers to stay and socialize. This emphasis on hospitality has been a key driver of Starbucks' success and has helped to create a strong emotional connection with its customers.

In addition to its focus on hospitality, Starbucks has also leveraged the power of retail to create a compelling in-store experience. The company has invested heavily in store design, creating a warm and inviting atmosphere that encourages customers to explore and discover new products. Starbucks also offers a wide range of merchandise, including coffee beans, teas, pastries, and branded items such as mugs and tumblers, which helps to drive incremental sales and strengthen customer loyalty.

Digital Integration: To further enhance its convergence strategy, Starbucks has also embraced digital technology to create a seamless and personalized customer experience. The company's mobile app, which allows customers to order and pay for their drinks in advance, has been a key driver of its digital success. The app also provides customers with personalized recommendations based on their purchase history and enables them to earn rewards and discounts.

In addition to its mobile app, Starbucks has also leveraged data analytics to gain insights into customer preferences and behaviour. By analyzing data from its loyalty program and mobile app, Starbucks has been able to optimize its menu offerings, store layouts, and promotional strategies to better meet the needs of its customers.

Impact and Results: Starbucks' convergence strategy has enabled the company to create a disruptive innovation that has transformed the coffee industry. By combining high-quality coffee, exceptional customer service, and a welcoming retail environment, Starbucks has been able to create a unique and compelling customer experience that has driven strong financial performance.

Red Bull

Convergence: Energy Drinks + Extreme Sports + Media

Red Bull, an Austrian company founded in 1987, has revolutionized the beverage industry by leveraging the convergence of energy drinks, extreme sports, and media. What started as a single product, the Red Bull energy drink, has grown into a global brand that is synonymous with adventure, excitement, and pushing the limits of human performance.

Convergence Strategy: Red Bull's convergence strategy is centered on the integration of its energy drink with the world of extreme sports and the creation of compelling media content. By combining elements from these different industries, Red Bull has been able to differentiate itself from competitors and create a powerful brand identity that resonates with consumers around the world.

At the core of Red Bull's convergence strategy is its focus on extreme sports. The company has long been a supporter of athletes and events in sports such as skateboarding, snowboarding, surfing, and motorsports. By aligning its brand with the excitement and adrenaline of these sports, Red Bull has been able to create a strong emotional connection with its target audience of young, adventurous consumers.

In addition to its support of extreme sports, Red Bull has also heavily invested in the creation of compelling media content. The company has its own media production arm, Red Bull Media House, which creates and distributes a wide range of content across multiple platforms, including television, film, digital, and print. This content, which includes documentaries, TV shows, and live events, helps to deepen the connection between Red Bull and its audience and provides a powerful platform for showcasing the brand's values and personality.

Event Activation: One of the key ways that Red Bull has leveraged its convergence strategy is through the creation and activation of its own events. The company has created a series of signature events, such as the Red Bull Cliff Diving World Series, the Red Bull Air Race, and the Red Bull Rampage, which bring together the worlds of extreme sports and media in a powerful and compelling way.

These events not only provide a platform for Red Bull to showcase its brand and products but also generate significant media coverage and social media buzz. By creating its own events, Red Bull has been able to control the narrative around its brand and create a powerful sense of exclusivity and desirability.

Red Bull's success serves as an inspiration and a roadmap for companies seeking to harness the power of industry convergence in their own pursuit of growth and competitive advantage.

In conclusion, industry convergence is a powerful driver of disruptive innovation in today's rapidly evolving business landscape. By combining elements from different sectors, companies can create new market opportunities, differentiate themselves from competitors, and deliver unprecedented value to customers.

To successfully leverage industry convergence, companies must adopt a proactive and strategic approach to innovation, fostering cross-functional collaboration, developing strategic partnerships, and embracing agility and experimentation.

As the boundaries between industries continue to blur, the ability to identify and capitalize on convergence opportunities will be a critical determinant of success in the future. Companies that can effectively navigate the challenges and harness the power of industry convergence will be well-positioned to drive disruptive innovation and shape the markets of tomorrow.

* * *

13

Circular Economy

In recent years, the Circular Economy has emerged as a powerful concept that challenges traditional linear models of production and consumption. By focusing on minimizing waste and maximizing the reuse and recycling of resources, the Circular Economy offers a framework for creating disruptive innovations that are both environmentally sustainable and economically viable. This chapter will explore how companies can leverage the principles of the Circular Economy to create disruptive innovations and gain a competitive advantage in the market.

Understanding the Circular Economy: To understand how the Circular Economy can drive disruptive innovation, it is first necessary to understand the limitations of the traditional linear economy, which is based on a "take-make-dispose" model. The Circular Economy, in contrast, is based on three key principles: designing out waste and pollution, keeping products and materials in use, and regenerating natural systems. By adopting these principles, companies can create disruptive innovations that are more sustainable, efficient, and profitable.

Designing for the Circular Economy: One of the key ways that companies can create disruptive innovations using the Circular Economy is by designing products and processes that are optimized for circularity. This involves designing products that are durable, reusable, and easily recyclable, as well as choosing sustainable materials and production processes. By implementing modular and adaptable design strategies, companies can create products that can be easily upgraded, repaired, and repurposed, extending their lifecycle and reducing waste.

Developing Circular Business Models: Another way that companies can create disruptive innovations using the Circular Economy is by developing new business models that prioritize access over ownership. This can include product-as-a-service models, where customers pay for the use of a product rather than owning it outright, as well as rental and leasing models. Collaborative consumption and sharing models, such as peer-to-peer platforms for sharing resources, can also help to reduce waste and maximize the utilization of assets.

Leveraging Technology for Circular Innovation: Technology can play a key role in enabling circular innovation by providing new tools and platforms for optimizing resource use, reducing waste, and creating new value propositions. For example, companies can use IoT sensors and big data analytics to monitor and optimize the performance of products and processes in real time. AI and machine learning can be used to predict when maintenance or repairs will be needed, reducing downtime and extending the lifecycle of products. Blockchain technology can be used to create transparent and traceable supply chains, enabling companies to ensure the sustainability and circularity of their products.

Building Circular Ecosystems and Partnerships: Finally, creating disruptive innovations using the Circular Economy often requires building collaborative ecosystems and partnerships that span the entire value chain. This can involve working with suppliers and partners to develop closed-loop systems for recycling and reusing resources, as well as engaging customers and stakeholders in circular initiatives. Participating in circular innovation networks and platforms can also help companies share knowledge, resources, and best practices, accelerating the development and adoption of circular solutions.

Philips

In 2014, Philips launched its "Circular Lighting" program, which aims to create value through circular design, business models, and supply chains in the lighting industry. As part of this initiative, Philips has developed a range of innovative products and services that prioritize circularity and sustainability.

One key example is Philips' "Light as a Service" (LaaS) model, which disrupts the traditional model of selling lighting products by offering lighting as a service instead. Under this model, Philips retains ownership of the lighting equipment and is responsible for its maintenance, repair, and replacement. Customers pay a regular fee for the lighting service, which includes the design, installation, and optimization of the lighting system.

The LaaS model aligns with the principles of the Circular Economy in several ways. First, it incentivizes Philips to design long-lasting, energy-efficient, and easily maintainable lighting products, as the company remains responsible for the products throughout their lifecycle. Second, it encourages the reuse and refurbishment of lighting equipment, as Philips can take back and upgrade products at the end of each contract. Finally, it enables the implementation of intelligent, data-driven lighting systems that can optimize energy use and minimize waste.

Philips has also leveraged technology to enable circular innovation in its lighting products. For example, the company has developed connected LED lighting systems that can be remotely monitored and controlled using IoT sensors and data analytics. This allows for real-time optimization of lighting performance, predictive maintenance, and easy upgrades or replacements of components.

In addition to its LaaS model and connected lighting systems, Philips has also worked to build circular ecosystems and partnerships across the lighting value chain. The company has collaborated with suppliers to develop closed-loop recycling systems for lighting components, as well as with customers and stakeholders to create tailored circular lighting solutions for specific industries and applications.

Philips' "Circular Lighting" program has been a success, generating new revenue streams, reducing environmental impact, and establishing the company as a leader in circular innovation. The program has also inspired other companies in the lighting industry and beyond to adopt circular principles and develop their own disruptive innovations.

Patagonia

Patagonia has long been known for its commitment to environmental sustainability, and in recent years, the company has embraced the Circular Economy as a key strategy for driving innovation and reducing its environmental impact.

One of Patagonia's most notable circular initiatives is its "Worn Wear" program, which encourages customers to repair, reuse, and recycle their Patagonia clothing and gear. Through the program, customers can bring their used Patagonia items to a store for repair, or trade them in for credit towards new purchases. Patagonia then cleans, repairs, and resells the used items at a discount, giving them a second life and keeping them out of landfills.

The "Worn Wear" program is a disruptive innovation that challenges the traditional linear model of clothing consumption, where products are bought, used, and then discarded. By prioritizing durability, repairability, and reuse, Patagonia is creating a circular ecosystem that reduces waste, conserves resources, and creates value for both the company and its customers.

In addition to the "Worn Wear" program, Patagonia has also implemented circular design principles across its product lines. The company uses high-quality, long-lasting materials and construction techniques to ensure that its products can withstand years of use and repair. Patagonia has also experimented with innovative materials, such as recycled polyester and organic cotton, to reduce its environmental footprint and close the loop on material use.

Patagonia has also leveraged technology to enable circular innovation in its supply chain. The company has implemented a number of digital tools and platforms, such as the "Footprint Chronicles," which provide transparency and traceability for its products from raw materials to finished goods. By using technology to monitor and optimize its supply chain, Patagonia can identify opportunities for circularity, such as recycling materials or reducing waste.

Finally, Patagonia has worked to build circular ecosystems and partnerships across the outdoor industry. The company has collaborated with other brands, suppliers, and non-profit organizations to develop industry-wide standards and initiatives for circularity, such as the "Sustainable Apparel Coalition" and the "Circular Economy 100."

Patagonia's circular initiatives have not only helped to reduce the company's environmental impact but have also driven business success. The "Worn Wear" program, for example, has created a new revenue stream for the company while also building customer loyalty and brand affinity.

In conclusion, the Circular Economy offers a powerful framework for creating disruptive innovations that are both environmentally sustainable and economically viable. By designing products and processes for circularity, developing new business models, leveraging technology, and building collaborative ecosystems, companies can create value in new and innovative ways, while also contributing to a more sustainable and resilient future. As the world faces growing environmental and resource challenges, the Circular Economy is likely to become an increasingly important driver of disruptive innovation in the years to come.

* * *

14

Shared Economy

The Shared Economy, also known as the Sharing Economy or Collaborative Consumption, has emerged as a powerful force for disruptive innovation in recent years. By enabling the sharing of underutilized assets and resources through digital platforms, the Shared Economy is creating new business models, disrupting traditional industries, and driving economic and social change. This chapter will explore how companies can leverage the principles of the Shared Economy to create disruptive innovations and unlock new sources of value.

Understanding the Shared Economy: To understand how the Shared Economy can drive disruptive innovation, it is first necessary to understand the key drivers and principles behind this emerging economic model. The Shared Economy is enabled by digital platforms and peer-to-peer marketplaces that allow individuals and businesses to share assets and resources, such as cars, homes, skills, and time. This shift from ownership to access is creating new opportunities for businesses to generate revenue, reduce costs, and create value for customers.

Identifying Opportunities for Shared Economy: To create disruptive innovations using the Shared Economy, companies must first identify opportunities for sharing and collaboration within their industry. This involves analyzing underutilized assets and resources, such as empty office space, idle equipment, or unused inventory, and identifying ways to share or monetize these assets through digital platforms. Companies should also look for pain points and inefficiencies in traditional business models, such as high transaction costs, limited access, or lack of flexibility, and explore how the Shared Economy can address these challenges. Finally, companies should consider new market segments and customer needs that may be underserved by traditional offerings and explore how the Shared Economy can create value for these segments.

Developing Shared Economy Business Models: Once opportunities for Shared Economy disruption have been identified, companies must develop new business models that leverage the principles of sharing and collaboration. Platform-based business models, such as Airbnb and Uber, use digital platforms to connect supply and demand and enable the sharing of assets and resources. Peer-to-peer marketplaces, such as Etsy and TaskRabbit, allow individuals to share their skills, expertise, and resources directly with each other. On-demand service models, such as Instacart and Postmates, provide access to services and expertise on an as-needed basis.

Building Trust and Reputation in the Shared Economy: One of the key challenges in the Shared Economy is building trust and ensuring the quality and safety of shared assets and transactions. To address this challenge, companies must implement robust rating and review systems that allow participants to provide feedback and establish their reputation. Companies must also develop verification and screening processes to ensure that participants are who they say they are and have the necessary skills and qualifications. Finally, companies must provide insurance and protection for shared assets and transactions to mitigate risks and create a sense of security for participants.

Navigating Regulatory and Legal Challenges in the Shared Economy: The Shared Economy is disrupting traditional industries and creating new regulatory and legal challenges for businesses and policymakers. To navigate these challenges, companies must first understand the local regulations and legal requirements that apply to their business model and ensure compliance. Companies should also work proactively with policymakers and regulators to create a supportive environment for the Shared Economy and address concerns around issues such as taxation, labor rights, and consumer protection. Finally, companies should collaborate with industry partners to develop self-regulatory frameworks and standards that promote best practices and ensure the long-term sustainability of the Shared Economy.

Leveraging Data and Analytics in the Shared Economy: Data and analytics play a critical role in the Shared Economy, enabling companies to optimize their platforms, personalize their offerings, and identify new opportunities for growth. By collecting and analyzing data on supply and demand patterns, user preferences, and transaction histories, companies can improve the efficiency and effectiveness of their matching algorithms and provide a better user experience. Companies can also use data to personalize their offerings and recommendations based on individual user needs and preferences. Finally, companies can leverage data to identify trends and opportunities for innovation and growth, such as expanding into new markets or developing new products and services.

Partnering and Collaborating in the Shared Economy: Creating disruptive innovations in the Shared Economy often requires partnering and collaborating with other businesses, communities, and stakeholders. By forming strategic partnerships with complementary businesses, such as transportation companies or hospitality providers, companies can expand their offerings and create new sources of value for customers. By collaborating with local communities and stakeholders, such as city governments or neighborhood associations, companies can build trust and support for their business models and address local concerns and needs. Finally, by participating in industry associations and networks, such as the Sharing Economy Association or the Collaborative Economy Coalition, companies can share best practices, advocate for supportive policies, and drive the overall growth and development of the Shared Economy.

TaskRabbit

Founded in 2008, TaskRabbit is an online marketplace that connects people who need help with household tasks and errands with skilled and vetted local freelancers known as "Taskers." TaskRabbit has disrupted the traditional home services industry by enabling the sharing of skills and labour and created a new market for on-demand task assistance.

TaskRabbit's business model is based on a platform that enables peer-to-peer transactions between Taskers and clients. Taskers can create profiles showcasing their skills and experience, set their own rates and availability, and bid on tasks posted by clients. Clients can browse Tasker profiles, read reviews from previous clients, and select the Tasker that best fits their needs and budget. TaskRabbit takes a service fee from each transaction as a commission to facilitate the connection and provide the platform.

One of the key factors in TaskRabbit's success has been its focus on trust and safety. The company has implemented a rigorous screening and vetting process for all Taskers, including background checks, identity verification, and in-person interviews. TaskRabbit also provides insurance and support for both Taskers and clients, helping to build trust and confidence in the platform.

TaskRabbit has also leveraged data and analytics to optimize its platform and create a better user experience. By analyzing data on task patterns, Tasker performance, and client preferences, TaskRabbit has been able to improve its matching algorithms, personalize its recommendations, and identify new opportunities for growth and expansion.

In addition to its core task assistance business, TaskRabbit has also formed strategic partnerships and collaborations to expand its offerings and reach new markets. For example, the company has partnered with major retailers such as IKEA and Walmart to provide furniture assembly and delivery services and with property management companies to offer move-in and move-out cleaning services.

The impact of TaskRabbit's disruptive innovation has been significant, both for the company itself and for the broader home services industry. TaskRabbit has grown steadily since its founding, with operations in over 50 cities in the United States and the United Kingdom. In 2017, the company was acquired by IKEA, one of its strategic partners, for an undisclosed sum.

At the same time, TaskRabbit's success has also inspired a wave of similar on-demand task assistance startups, such as Handy, Thumbtack, and Zaarly. These companies have helped to create a new market for flexible and accessible home services, challenging traditional providers such as home cleaning and handyman services.

Coursera

Founded in 2012, Coursera is an online learning platform that partners with top universities and organizations worldwide to offer courses, specializations, and degrees to learners everywhere. By leveraging the principles of the Shared Economy, Coursera has made high-quality education more accessible and affordable, disrupting the traditional higher education industry.

Coursera's business model is based on a platform that enables the sharing of educational content and expertise between universities, instructors, and learners. Universities and instructors can create and share courses on the platform, reaching a global audience of learners. Learners can access courses on a wide range of subjects, from computer science and data analytics to business and the humanities, and earn certificates or degrees upon completion. Coursera generates revenue through a variety of means, including course fees, subscription plans, and partnerships with employers and organizations.

One of the key factors in Coursera's success has been its ability to partner with top universities and organizations to offer high-quality educational content. The company has formed partnerships with over 200 universities and organizations, including Stanford, Yale, Google, and IBM, to create courses and programs that are relevant and valuable to learners and employers. By leveraging the expertise and brand recognition of these partners, Coursera has been able to attract a large and diverse audience of learners from around the world.

Coursera has also leveraged data and analytics to optimize its platform and create a personalized learning experience for each user. By analyzing data on learner behaviour, preferences, and performance, Coursera has been able to improve its recommendation algorithms, adaptive learning features, and course content. The company has also used data to identify skills gaps and job market trends, partnering with employers to create courses and programs that help learners acquire in-demand skills and advance their careers.

In addition to its core online learning business, Coursera has also expanded into new markets and services through strategic partnerships and initiatives. For example, the company has partnered with governments and non-profit organizations to provide job training and reskilling programs for underserved communities and with employers to offer corporate learning solutions for workforce development. Coursera has also launched new products and services, such as Coursera for Campus, which enables universities to use Coursera's platform and content to create blended and online learning programs for their students.

The impact of Coursera's disruptive innovation has been significant, both for the company itself and for the broader education and workforce development industries. Coursera has grown rapidly since its founding, with over 77 million registered learners and 5,000 courses and specializations offered by over 200 university and industry partners. The company has also raised over $460 million in funding from top investors, including NEA, Kleiner Perkins, and Future Fund.

At the same time, Coursera's success has also created new challenges and opportunities for traditional higher education institutions. Many universities have responded by partnering with Coursera and other online learning platforms to expand their reach and offerings, while also investing in their own online and blended learning programs. The rise of online learning has also sparked new conversations and debates around the future of higher education, including issues of access, affordability, and quality.

In conclusion, the Shared Economy offers a powerful framework for creating disruptive innovations that unlock new sources of value and drive economic and social change. By leveraging the principles of sharing and collaboration, developing new business models, building trust and reputation, navigating regulatory and legal challenges, leveraging data and analytics, and partnering and collaborating with others, companies can create disruptive innovations that challenge traditional industries and create a more sustainable and equitable future. As the Shared Economy continues to evolve and mature, it is likely to become an increasingly important driver of innovation and growth in the years to come.

* * *

15

Gamification

Gamification has emerged as a powerful tool for driving engagement, motivation, and innovation in a wide range of industries and contexts. By applying game-design elements and principles to non-game contexts, companies can create more engaging and effective experiences for customers, employees, and stakeholders.

Understanding Gamification: To understand how gamification can drive disruptive innovation, it is important to first understand the psychology of gameplay and motivation. Games are inherently engaging and motivating because they tap into fundamental human desires for achievement, competition, collaboration, and self-expression. By understanding these psychological drivers, companies can design gamified experiences that are more effective at engaging and motivating users.

The key elements of game design include points, badges, leaderboards, challenges, and rewards. These elements can be used in various combinations to create gamified experiences that are tailored to specific goals and audiences. When applied effectively, gamification can lead to increased engagement, loyalty, and motivation, as well as improved learning, productivity, and innovation.

Identifying Opportunities for Gamification: To identify opportunities for gamification, companies should start by analyzing customer and employee pain points and motivations. What are the key challenges and obstacles that users face, and what motivates them to engage with a product, service, or experience? By understanding these factors, companies can identify areas where gamification can have the greatest impact.

Companies should also assess the potential impact and feasibility of gamification for each opportunity. What are the goals and objectives of the gamified experience, and how will success be measured? What resources and capabilities are required to design and implement the gamified experience, and what are the potential risks and challenges?

Designing Gamified Experiences: Once opportunities for gamification have been identified, companies can begin designing gamified experiences that are tailored to specific goals and audiences. The first step is to define clear goals and objectives for the gamified experience, such as increasing user engagement, driving product adoption, or improving employee performance.

Next, companies should select appropriate game elements and mechanics that align with these goals and objectives. This may include points, badges, leaderboards, challenges, and rewards, as well as more advanced elements such as social interaction, storytelling, and personalization.

Creating a compelling narrative and theme is also important for engaging users and creating a sense of purpose and meaning. The narrative should be consistent with the goals and objectives of the gamified experience and should be integrated into the overall design.

Balancing challenge and reward is another key aspect of designing effective gamified experiences. The challenges should be difficult enough to be engaging and motivating, but not so difficult that they become frustrating or discouraging. Rewards should be meaningful and valuable to users and should be tied to specific achievements and milestones.

Finally, iterating and testing the design is essential for ensuring that the gamified experience is effective and engaging. Companies should gather feedback from users and stakeholders and use this feedback to refine and improve the design over time.

Implementing and Managing Gamified Experiences: Implementing and managing gamified experiences requires careful planning and execution. Companies should start by integrating gamification into existing products and processes, rather than treating it as a separate initiative. This may require modifications to existing systems and workflows, as well as training and support for users and stakeholders.

Measuring and analyzing performance and engagement is also critical for ensuring the success of gamified experiences. Companies should define key metrics and KPIs that align with the goals and objectives of the gamified experience and should regularly track and report on these metrics. This data can be used to identify areas for improvement and to optimize the gamified experience over time.

Adapting and optimizing the gamified experience based on user feedback and performance data is an ongoing process. Companies should be prepared to make changes and adjustments to the design and implementation of the gamified experience as needed to ensure that it remains engaging and effective over time.

Examples of Gamification in Action

Nike+ Run Club (NRC)

Nike, a global leader in athletic footwear and apparel, disrupted the fitness industry by introducing the Nike+ Run Club (NRC) app. The app uses gamification to transform the running experience and engage users in ways that traditional running apps did not.

1. **Goal Setting and Progress Tracking:** NRC allows users to set personalized running goals, such as distance, time, or frequency. The app tracks users' progress and provides real-time feedback during runs, keeping them motivated and engaged.
2. **Achievements and Rewards:** Users earn virtual medals, trophies, and

milestones for completing runs, reaching goals, and participating in challenges. These rewards create a sense of accomplishment and encourage users to continue using the app.
3. **Social Competition and Collaboration:** NRC enables users to connect with friends, join running communities, and participate in virtual races and challenges. Users can compete against each other, share their achievements on social media, and collaborate to reach common goals, fostering a sense of community and friendly competition.
4. **Personalized Coaching and Guidance:** The app offers personalized coaching plans adapted to each user's fitness level, goals, and schedule. Users receive audio guidance from professional coaches during runs, providing motivation and real-time feedback on their performance.
5. **Immersive Storytelling:** NRC features guided runs with immersive storytelling experiences, such as running through famous cities or alongside celebrity athletes. These experiences create a unique and engaging running environment that keeps users excited about their workouts.

By integrating gamification elements into the running experience, Nike has created a disruptive innovation that sets NRC apart from traditional running apps. The app has successfully engaged millions of users, increased brand loyalty, and established Nike as a leader in the digital fitness space. NRC's success has inspired other brands to incorporate gamification into their products and services, demonstrating the power of this strategy in driving disruptive innovation.

Disruptive vs Sustaining Innovation: Sustaining innovations are improvements to existing products or services that enhance performance, features, or value for the company's existing customer base. These innovations help companies maintain their competitive edge and meet the evolving needs of their current market.

In the case of NRC, it could be argued that the app is a sustaining innovation because:

1. It builds upon Nike's existing brand and products, targeting its current customer base of athletes and fitness enthusiasts.
2. The app enhances the running experience by providing features that complement Nike's core offering of athletic footwear and apparel.

On the other hand, disruptive innovations create new markets or reshape existing ones by offering solutions that are simpler, more convenient, or more affordable than existing offerings. Disruptive innovations often target underserved or overlooked markets and can eventually displace established competitors.

From this perspective, NRC could be considered a disruptive innovation because:

1. It targets a broader market of casual runners and fitness enthusiasts who may not have been part of Nike's traditional customer base. By making running more engaging, Nike+ potentially opened it up to a wider audience who might not have found it appealing otherwise.
2. It created a new way for runners to interact with the brand and the activity itself. The gamified experience wasn't something traditional running shoes offered. It potentially displaces them in the market.
3. NRC has the potential to create a new market for digitally-enhanced running experiences, challenging the status quo of the fitness industry.

Ultimately, the classification of NRC as a sustaining or disruptive innovation depends on the perspective and the context in which it is analyzed. It is essential to consider the app's impact on the market, its target audience, and its potential to reshape the industry when determining its innovation type. In some cases, an innovation may have characteristics of both sustaining and disruptive innovation, making it a hybrid of the two.

Duolingo

Duolingo is a language learning platform that has disrupted the traditional language education industry by offering a gamified, accessible, and engaging approach to learning new languages.

1. **Bite-sized Lessons:** Duolingo breaks down language learning into small, manageable lessons that users can complete in short bursts. Each lesson is designed as a mini-game, with interactive exercises that test reading, writing, speaking, and listening skills. This approach makes language learning less intimidating and more enjoyable for users.
2. **Progress Tracking and Rewards:** The app uses a gamified system of experience points (XP), levels, and achievements to track users' progress and keep them motivated. Users earn XP for completing lessons, maintaining daily streaks, and achieving specific milestones. As they level up, they unlock new content and features, creating a sense of progression and accomplishment.
3. **Competitive Leaderboards:** Duolingo introduces a competitive element by allowing users to join leaderboards and compete against friends or other learners worldwide. This feature taps into users' competitive nature and encourages them to engage with the app more frequently to climb the ranks.
4. **Social Sharing and Collaboration:** Users can connect with friends, share their progress on social media, and engage in friendly competitions. Duolingo also offers community features, such as forums and language clubs, where learners can interact with native speakers, ask questions, and practice their language skills in a supportive environment.
5. **Adaptive Learning:** Duolingo uses machine learning algorithms to personalize the learning experience for each user. The app adapts to users' strengths and weaknesses, focusing on areas that need improvement and providing targeted feedback to help them progress more effectively.

By gamifying the language learning experience, Duolingo has disrupted the traditional language education market in several ways:

1. **Accessibility:** Duolingo offers a free, mobile-first platform that makes language learning accessible to a wider audience, including those who may not have the time, resources, or means to attend traditional language classes.
2. **Engagement:** The gamified approach keeps users engaged and motivated to continue learning, reducing the high dropout rates often associated with traditional language courses.
3. **Effectiveness:** Duolingo's adaptive learning algorithms and bite-sized lessons have proven effective in helping users acquire language skills, challenging the notion that language learning requires intensive, classroom-based instruction.

Duolingo's disruptive innovation has not only attracted millions of users worldwide but has also inspired other edutech companies to incorporate gamification into their learning platforms. By making language learning more engaging, accessible, and effective, Duolingo has reshaped the language education landscape and created a new market for gamified learning experiences.

Challenges and Limitations of Gamification: While gamification can be a powerful tool for driving innovation and success, it is not without its challenges and limitations. One of the main challenges is overcoming resistance and scepticism from users and stakeholders who may view gamification as frivolous or manipulative. Companies must be transparent about the goals and benefits of gamification and must ensure that the gamified experience is genuinely engaging and valuable to users.

Another challenge is ensuring long-term engagement and motivation. While gamification can be effective at driving short-term engagement and behaviour change, sustaining this engagement over time can be more difficult. Companies must continually adapt and optimize the gamified experience to ensure that it remains relevant and engaging to users.

Avoiding unintended consequences and negative behaviours is also important. Poorly designed gamified experiences can lead to unintended consequences such as cheating, gaming the system, or neglecting other important priorities. Companies must carefully design and test gamified experiences to ensure that they promote positive behaviors and outcomes.

Finally, balancing gamification with other priorities and constraints can be challenging. Gamification should not be viewed as a silver bullet or a replacement for other important strategies and initiatives. Companies must carefully consider how gamification fits into their overall business strategy and must ensure that it is aligned with other priorities and constraints.

The Future of Gamification and Disruptive Innovation: Looking to the future, it is clear that gamification will continue to play an important role in driving disruptive innovation and business success. As more companies and organizations adopt gamification and as the technologies and techniques for creating gamified experiences continue to evolve, we can expect to see even more sophisticated and effective examples of gamification in action.

One exciting area of potential for gamification is in driving social and environmental impact. By gamifying behaviours and activities that promote sustainability, social responsibility, and other important values, companies and organizations can use gamification to create positive change in the world.

At the same time, the increasing prevalence of gamification also highlights the need for responsible and ethical gamification practices. Companies must be transparent about their use of gamification and must ensure that gamified experiences are designed in a way that respects user privacy, autonomy, and well-being.

Finally, as gamification continues to evolve and mature, we can expect to see new opportunities for gamification to enable new forms of innovation and value creation. By leveraging the power of game design to engage and motivate users in new and creative ways, companies and organizations can unlock new sources of value and drive disruptive innovation in a wide range of industries and contexts.

In conclusion, gamification offers a powerful tool for creating disruptive innovation and driving business success. By understanding the psychology of gameplay and motivation, identifying opportunities for gamification, designing effective gamified experiences, and managing and optimizing these experiences over time, companies can create engaging and impactful experiences that drive innovation and value creation. As the world becomes increasingly complex and competitive, gamification will likely play an even greater role in shaping the future of business and society.

***

16

Reverse Innovation

Reverse innovation is a strategy that involves developing products or services specifically for emerging markets, with the intention of later introducing them to developed markets. This approach challenges the traditional notion of innovation, which typically flows from developed to emerging markets. By focusing on the unique needs, constraints, and preferences of consumers in emerging markets, companies can create disruptive innovations that not only succeed in these markets but also have the potential to disrupt established markets.

1. **Identifying Unmet Needs:** The first step in reverse innovation is to identify the unmet needs and pain points of consumers in emerging markets. These needs may differ significantly from those in developed markets due to factors such as income levels, cultural preferences, and infrastructure limitations. Companies must conduct thorough market research and engage with local communities to gain a deep understanding of these needs and how they can be addressed.
2. **Designing for Constraints:** Emerging markets often present unique constraints, such as limited purchasing power, unreliable infrastructure, and varying cultural norms. To create successful reverse innovations, companies must design products and services that can operate within these constraints. This may involve developing more affordable, durable,

and easy-to-use solutions that can function in challenging environments.

3. **Local Partnerships and Collaboration:** Collaborating with local partners, including suppliers, distributors, and community organizations, is crucial for successful reverse innovation. These partnerships provide valuable insights into local market dynamics, help navigate cultural and regulatory challenges, and ensure that innovations are tailored to the specific needs of the target market. Local collaborations also help build trust and credibility with consumers.

4. **Frugal Engineering:** Reverse innovation often requires a frugal engineering approach, which focuses on creating high-value, low-cost solutions. This involves simplifying product designs, using locally available materials, and optimizing manufacturing processes to reduce costs without compromising quality. Frugal engineering enables companies to offer affordable products that meet the needs of price-sensitive consumers in emerging markets.

5. **Adaptability and Scalability:** Successful reverse innovations must be adaptable and scalable. As products and services gain traction in emerging markets, companies should be prepared to iterate and refine their offerings based on customer feedback and changing market conditions. Additionally, innovations should be designed with scalability in mind, allowing for easy expansion into other emerging markets or adaptation for developed markets.

6. **Reverse Flow of Innovation:** Once reverse innovations have proven successful in emerging markets, companies can consider introducing them to developed markets. This reverse flow of innovation can disrupt established markets by offering more affordable, accessible, and tailored solutions. Reverse innovations may need to be adapted to meet the specific requirements and preferences of developed markets, but their proven success in emerging markets can provide a strong foundation for entry.

Vscan by GE Healthcare

In the early 2000s, GE Healthcare recognized that traditional ultrasound machines were not meeting the needs of healthcare providers in emerging markets like India. These machines were often bulky, expensive, and required reliable electricity and trained operators, making them inaccessible to many healthcare facilities in rural and remote areas. GE Healthcare saw an opportunity to create a disruptive innovation that could address these challenges and improve access to ultrasound technology in underserved markets.

The Solution: GE Healthcare's engineers in India and China set out to design a portable, affordable, and easy-to-use ultrasound machine specifically for the needs of emerging markets. The result was Vscan, a handheld device about the size of a smartphone that could perform basic ultrasound scans and provide real-time imaging.

Key features of Vscan:

1. **Portability:** Vscan's compact size and light weight made it easy for healthcare providers to carry the device to remote locations and perform scans at the point of care.
2. **Affordability:** By simplifying the design, using off-the-shelf components, and manufacturing locally, GE Healthcare was able to offer Vscan at a fraction of the cost of traditional ultrasound machines, making it more accessible to healthcare facilities with limited budgets.
3. **Ease of use:** Vscan featured a simple, intuitive interface that required minimal training to operate, enabling healthcare workers with basic skills to perform ultrasound scans and interpret the results.
4. **Battery-powered:** Vscan could operate on battery power, making it suitable for use in areas with unreliable electricity supply.

Impact in Emerging Markets: Vscan's introduction to the Indian market was a game-changer. The device empowered healthcare providers in rural and remote areas to perform basic ultrasound scans, improving diagnostic capabilities and patient outcomes. Vscan's success in India led GE Healthcare to expand its reach to other emerging markets, including China, Africa, and Latin America, where it continued to make a significant impact on healthcare access and quality.

Reverse Flow to Developed Markets: As Vscan gained traction in emerging markets, GE Healthcare recognized its potential to disrupt developed markets as well. In 2010, the company introduced Vscan to the United States and other developed markets, positioning it as a convenient, portable, and affordable solution for point-of-care ultrasound.

In developed markets, Vscan found applications in various settings, including:

1. **Emergency medicine:** Vscan enabled quick bedside assessments in emergency departments, helping healthcare providers make faster diagnoses and treatment decisions.
2. **Primary care:** General practitioners and family physicians used Vscan to perform basic ultrasound scans during office visits, reducing the need for referrals to specialized imaging centres.
3. **Medical education:** Vscan served as a valuable teaching tool, allowing medical students and trainees to gain hands-on experience with ultrasound technology.

GE Healthcare's Vscan disrupted the ultrasound industry by challenging the notion that ultrasound machines had to be large, expensive, and complex. By focusing on the needs of emerging markets and designing a portable, affordable, and user-friendly solution, GE Healthcare created a product that not only succeeded in its intended market but also found a place in developed markets, expanding access to ultrasound technology and improving patient care.

UPI Payments

In 2016, the National Payments Corporation of India (NPCI) launched UPI, a real-time payment system that facilitates inter-bank transactions through mobile devices. UPI was developed to address the challenges faced by the Indian population, such as limited access to banking services, a high reliance on cash transactions, and the need for a secure, convenient, and affordable digital payment solution.

The UPI Solution: UPI is a mobile-first, real-time payment system that allows users to send and receive money instantly using their mobile devices. It operates as a single interface for all bank accounts, enabling seamless transactions across different banks and payment apps.

Key features of UPI:

1. **Interoperability:** UPI allows users to link multiple bank accounts to a single mobile app, enabling transactions across different banks and payment platforms. This interoperability makes it convenient for users to manage their finances and conduct transactions without the need for multiple apps or interfaces.
2. **Affordability:** UPI transactions are cost-effective, with minimal or no transaction fees. This affordability has made digital payments accessible to a wide range of users, including those from lower-income segments.
3. **Ease of use:** UPI offers a simple and intuitive user interface, making it easy for users to adopt digital payments. Transactions can be initiated using virtual payment addresses (VPAs) or QR codes, eliminating the need to share sensitive bank account details.
4. **Security:** UPI incorporates robust security measures, such as two-factor authentication and end-to-end encryption, to ensure the safety of user transactions and data.

UPI has revolutionized the digital payment landscape in India. It has brought millions of previously underbanked and unbanked individuals into the formal financial system, driving financial inclusion. The ease, affordability, and security of UPI have made it the preferred payment method for a wide range of transactions, from peer-to-peer transfers to merchant payments.

The success of UPI can be attributed to several factors:

1. **Government support:** The Indian government has actively promoted the adoption of UPI and other digital payment solutions through initiatives like "Digital India". This support has created a conducive environment for the growth of digital payments.
2. **Collaboration with tech giants:** NPCI has partnered with tech giants like Google, Amazon, and Walmart-owned PhonePe to integrate UPI into their payment platforms. These collaborations have expanded UPI's reach and made it more accessible to users.
3. **Localized solutions:** UPI has been designed to address the specific needs and challenges of the Indian market, such as the prevalence of feature phones and limited internet connectivity. This localization has made UPI more relevant and adoptable for Indian users.

Potential for Reverse Innovation: The success of UPI in India has attracted global attention, with several countries exploring the possibility of implementing similar digital payment solutions. The UPI model, with its focus on interoperability, affordability, and ease of use, has the potential to disrupt traditional payment systems in developed markets.

Some key aspects of UPI that could drive reverse innovation include:

1. **Cost-effectiveness:** UPI's low transaction fees could challenge the high costs associated with traditional payment methods in developed markets, making digital payments more accessible and affordable.
2. **Interoperability:** The seamless integration of different banks and payment platforms through UPI could inspire similar models in developed markets, breaking down silos and promoting competition.
3. **Financial inclusion:** UPI's success in bringing underbanked and unbanked populations into the formal financial system could provide valuable insights for developed markets looking to expand financial

inclusion.

While the specific implementation of UPI in developed markets may require adaptations to suit local regulations and infrastructure, the core principles and features of UPI have the potential to drive disruptive innovation in the global digital payment landscape.

By embracing reverse innovation, companies can tap into the vast potential of emerging markets, create disruptive innovations that challenge established norms, and unlock new opportunities for growth and expansion. As the global business landscape continues to evolve, reverse innovation will likely play an increasingly important role in driving disruptive innovation and reshaping industries.

* * *

17

Breaking Functional Fixedness

In the pursuit of disruptive innovation, organizations often focus on external factors such as market trends, emerging technologies, and changing customer needs. However, one of the biggest barriers to innovation lies within our own minds: functional fixedness. Functional fixedness is a cognitive bias that limits our ability to see objects or concepts beyond their traditional or intended uses. It's a mental block that hinders creativity and prevents us from recognizing the full potential of the resources at our disposal.

The Limitations of Functional Fixedness

Functional fixedness is a common cognitive bias that affects individuals and organizations alike. It occurs when we become so familiar with an object or concept that we struggle to see it in a new light or imagine alternative uses for it. For example, if you've always used a paperclip to hold papers together, you might not consider its potential as a makeshift lock pick or a tool for resetting electronic devices.

In the context of innovation, functional fixedness can be a major hindrance. It can limit our ability to see the full potential of existing products, technologies, or business models, and prevent us from exploring new and innovative applications. This is particularly true in industries where established practices and ways of thinking have become entrenched over time.

Consider the example of Blockbuster, the once-dominant video rental chain. Blockbuster was so fixated on its traditional brick-and-mortar business model that it failed to recognize the disruptive potential of online streaming services like Netflix. By the time Blockbuster finally adapted to the changing market, it was too late – the company filed for bankruptcy in 2010.

Strategies for Breaking Functional Fixedness

To create truly disruptive innovation, organizations must find ways to break free from the constraints of functional fixedness. Here are five strategies that can help:

Encourage Diverse Perspectives: One of the most effective ways to break functional fixedness is to bring together individuals with diverse backgrounds, experiences, and perspectives. When people with different viewpoints collaborate, they can challenge each other's assumptions and generate new and innovative ideas.

For example, when designing its innovative Swiffer mop, Procter & Gamble brought together a team of engineers, designers, and marketers from different parts of the company. By combining their diverse expertise, the team was able to create a product that revolutionized the cleaning industry and generated over $500 million in sales in its first year.

Promote Experimentation and Play: Another way to break functional fixedness is to create an environment that encourages experimentation and play. When individuals feel free to explore and tinker with ideas without fear of failure, they're more likely to come up with novel and innovative solutions.

Google is famous for its "20% time" policy, which allows employees to spend one day a week working on projects of their own choosing. This policy has led to the development of some of Google's most successful products, including Gmail and AdSense.

Reframe Problems and Challenges: Sometimes, the key to breaking functional fixedness is to reframe the problem or challenge at hand. By looking at a situation from a different angle or asking "what if" questions, we can open up new possibilities and generate innovative solutions.

For example, when developing the Swiffer mop, Procter & Gamble initially focused on creating a better mop. However, by reframing the problem as "how can we make cleaning floors easier and more convenient," the team was able to develop a product that was entirely different from traditional mops.

Embrace Constraints and Limitations: While it may seem counterintuitive, embracing constraints and limitations can actually stimulate creativity and innovation. When faced with limited resources or tight deadlines, individuals are forced to think outside the box and come up with novel solutions.

Consider the example of Southwest Airlines, which has built a successful business model around the constraint of using only one type of aircraft (the Boeing 737). By standardizing its fleet, Southwest has been able to reduce costs, simplify maintenance, and offer low fares to customers.

Foster a Culture of Curiosity and Continuous Learning: Finally, organizations can break functional fixedness by fostering a culture of curiosity and continuous learning. When employees are encouraged to ask questions, challenge assumptions, and seek out new knowledge and skills, they're more likely to generate innovative ideas and solutions.

3M is well-known for its culture of innovation, which is built on a foundation of curiosity and continuous learning. The company encourages employees to spend 15% of their time exploring new ideas and collaborating with colleagues from different departments.

3M Post-it Notes

In 1968, Dr. Spencer Silver, a chemist at 3M, was attempting to develop a strong adhesive for use in aerospace applications. However, he accidentally created a weak adhesive that could be easily peeled off surfaces without leaving any residue. While this "failure" did not meet the original objective, Dr. Silver recognized that his discovery might have other potential applications.

Enter Art Fry, a colleague of Dr Silver at 3M, who was frustrated with the way his paper bookmarks kept falling out of his hymnal during choir practice. Fry realized that Dr. Silver's weak adhesive could be the perfect solution to his bookmark problem.

By breaking the functional fixedness around the idea that an adhesive had to be strong and permanent, Fry and Silver were able to conceptualize a new product: a piece of paper with a strip of weak adhesive on the back that could be easily attached and removed from surfaces. This product, which came to be known as the Post-it Note, was initially met with scepticism within 3M, as it challenged the conventional notion of what an adhesive should be.

However, through persistent advocacy and creative marketing, Fry and Silver were able to convince 3M to launch the Post-it Note in 1980. The product quickly gained popularity, as consumers discovered the many uses for a small, repositionable piece of paper, from leaving reminders and messages to bookmarking and brainstorming.

By breaking the functional fixedness around adhesives and reconceptualizing the potential uses for a "failed" invention, 3M was able to create a disruptive innovation that transformed the office supply industry and became a ubiquitous part of modern life.

IKEA

Before IKEA entered the market, the furniture industry was characterized by bulky, expensive, and often inaccessible products. Furniture shopping was a time-consuming and costly endeavor, with limited options for the average consumer. Most furniture was sold pre-assembled, which made it difficult to transport and resulted in higher prices due to the cost of labor and shipping.

Breaking Functional Fixedness: IKEA's founder, Ingvar Kamprad, recognized an opportunity to challenge the traditional furniture industry by breaking the functional fixedness around how furniture was designed, manufactured, and sold. Instead of following the established model of selling pre-assembled, expensive furniture, Kamprad reimagined the entire process from the ground up.

The key to IKEA's disruptive innovation was the introduction of flat-pack, self-assembly furniture. By designing furniture that could be packed flat and assembled by the customer at home, IKEA was able to reduce costs, minimize transportation challenges, and offer a wider range of stylish and affordable products.

Implementing the Flat-Pack Revolution: IKEA's flat-pack furniture concept required a complete overhaul of the company's design and manufacturing processes. IKEA designers focused on creating furniture that could be easily disassembled and packed into compact, flat boxes. This approach required clever engineering and the use of standardized parts and materials, which streamlined production and reduced costs.

To support the self-assembly model, IKEA invested heavily in creating clear, visual instructions that could be easily followed by customers with minimal technical skills. The company also designed specialized tools and hardware that made assembly as straightforward as possible.

Transforming the Customer Experience: By breaking functional fixedness in the furniture industry, IKEA transformed the customer experience and made stylish, affordable furniture accessible to a broader audience. Customers could now browse a wide selection of furniture in-store or online, purchase their chosen items, and transport them home easily in their own vehicles.

The self-assembly aspect of IKEA's furniture not only empowered customers to take control of the process but also created a sense of accomplishment and ownership. Many customers found the experience of assembling their own furniture to be rewarding and even enjoyable.

Disrupting the Market: IKEA's flat-pack, self-assembly approach disrupted the traditional furniture retail market and forced competitors to adapt. The company's success demonstrated that there was significant demand for affordable, stylish furniture that could be easily transported and assembled by the customer.

As IKEA expanded globally, it continued to refine its business model and product offerings, always keeping the core principles of affordability, functionality, and accessibility at the forefront. The company's disruptive innovation not only changed the way furniture was sold but also influenced consumer expectations and behaviors around home furnishings.

In conclusion, breaking functional fixedness is a powerful strategy for creating disruptive innovation. By overcoming the mental barriers that limit our ability to see objects and concepts in new ways, we can unlock new possibilities and generate truly innovative ideas.

To break functional fixedness, organizations must foster a culture of diversity, experimentation, and continuous learning. They must encourage employees to challenge assumptions, reframe problems, and embrace constraints as opportunities for innovation.

So, the next time you find yourself stuck in a rut or struggling to come up with new ideas, remember the power of breaking functional fixedness. By opening your mind to new possibilities and embracing the strategies outlined in this chapter, you too can become a disruptive innovator and create the game-changing solutions that will shape the future.

* * *

18

Kill Your Own Business

In the relentless pursuit of disruptive innovation, organizations often focus on external threats and opportunities, overlooking the potential for disruption from within. The "Kill Your Own Business" strategy challenges companies to proactively cannibalize their existing products, services, and business models before competitors or new entrants do it for them.

The Paradox of Success

One of the biggest barriers to disruptive innovation is the success trap. When companies achieve success with a particular product, service, or business model, they often become complacent and risk-averse. They focus on protecting and optimizing their existing offerings, rather than exploring new and potentially disruptive opportunities. This mindset can lead to a gradual erosion of competitive advantage and leave organizations vulnerable to disruption from more agile and innovative players.

The "Kill Your Own Business" strategy challenges this conventional wisdom. It argues that companies must be willing to disrupt themselves before others do it for them. By proactively cannibalizing their own offerings and exploring new and innovative alternatives, organizations can stay ahead of the curve and maintain their competitive edge in an ever-changing business landscape.

The Self-Disruption Framework

To effectively implement the "Kill Your Own Business" strategy, organizations need a structured approach to self-disruption. The Self-Disruption Framework provides a roadmap for companies to systematically identify, evaluate, and pursue opportunities for self-disruption. The framework consists of four key stages:

1. **Identify the Threat:** The first step is to identify the potential threats to the organization's existing business. This involves a deep analysis of market trends, emerging technologies, changing customer needs, and competitive dynamics. By understanding the forces that could disrupt the business, companies can proactively plan for and respond to these challenges.

2. **Evaluate the Opportunity:** Once potential threats have been identified, the next step is to evaluate the opportunities for self-disruption. This involves assessing the feasibility, viability, and desirability of new products, services, or business models that could potentially cannibalize the existing business. By carefully weighing the risks and rewards of self-disruption, organizations can make informed decisions about which opportunities to pursue.

3. **Experiment and Iterate:** Self-disruption is an iterative process that requires experimentation and learning. Organizations should adopt a lean and agile approach to innovation, rapidly prototyping and testing new ideas and concepts. By embracing a culture of experimentation and failure, companies can quickly identify what works and what doesn't, and refine their self-disruption strategies accordingly.

4. **Scale and Integrate:** Once a promising self-disruption opportunity has been identified and validated through experimentation, the final step is to scale and integrate it into the organization's core business. This requires a careful balance between protecting the existing business and nurturing the new, disruptive offering. Organizations must be prepared to allocate resources, adapt their structures and processes, and manage

potential conflicts between the old and new businesses.

Overcoming Resistance to Self-Disruption

Implementing the "Kill Your Own Business" strategy is not without its challenges. Self-disruption can be met with resistance from various stakeholders, including employees, shareholders, and customers. Some common objections include:

1. **Cannibalization Concerns:** There may be fears that self-disruption will cannibalize the existing business and erode profitability. However, it is important to recognize that if the company doesn't disrupt itself, someone else will. By proactively cannibalizing its own offerings, the organization can control the process and capture the value from the new, disruptive business.
2. **Short-term Thinking:** Self-disruption often requires a long-term perspective and a willingness to sacrifice short-term profits for long-term gain. This can be challenging in a business environment that is often focused on quarterly results and immediate returns. Leaders must work to shift the mindset of the organization towards a more strategic and forward-looking approach.
3. **Organizational Inertia:** Established companies often have deeply entrenched cultures, processes, and structures that can hinder self-disruption. Overcoming this inertia requires strong leadership, clear communication, and a willingness to challenge the status quo. Leaders must be prepared to make tough decisions and drive change throughout the organization.
4. **Fear of Failure:** Self-disruption involves taking risks and embracing uncertainty. This can be uncomfortable for organizations that are used to operating within well-defined boundaries and predictable outcomes. Building a culture that celebrates experimentation and learns from failure is critical to overcoming this fear and fostering a more innovative mindset.

Apple and the iPhone

When Apple introduced the iPhone in 2007, it was a bold move that threatened to cannibalize the company's own iPod business, which at the time was a major source of revenue and growth. The iPod was a hugely successful product that revolutionized the portable music player market and established Apple as a leader in consumer electronics.

However, Apple recognized that the mobile phone market was ripe for disruption and that the convergence of mobile computing and communication represented a significant opportunity for growth. The iPhone was a revolutionary product that combined the functionality of a phone, a music player, and an internet-connected device in a single, sleek package.

By cannibalizing its own iPod business, Apple was able to create an entirely new market for smartphones and mobile applications. The iPhone quickly became a major source of revenue and growth for the company, far surpassing the iPod in terms of sales and profitability.

Apple's willingness to disrupt its own successful business and embrace a new and uncertain market is a prime example of the "Kill Your Own Business" strategy in action. The company recognized that the future of computing was mobile and that the iPhone represented a once-in-a-generation opportunity to redefine the industry and create new value for customers.

Today, the iPhone remains one of Apple's most important and profitable products, and the company continues to innovate and iterate on the platform to stay ahead of the competition.

Netflix and Streaming Video

Netflix began as a DVD-by-mail rental service in the late 1990s, offering customers a convenient and affordable alternative to traditional video rental stores. The company's business model was based on mailing physical DVDs to customers and charging a monthly subscription fee for unlimited rentals.

However, as the internet and broadband connectivity became more widespread in the mid-2000s, Netflix recognized that the future of video entertainment was online. The company began to invest heavily in streaming video technology and content licensing, even though it knew that streaming would eventually cannibalize its own DVD rental business.

In 2007, Netflix launched its streaming service, which allowed customers to watch movies and TV shows online without the need for physical DVDs. The service was an instant hit, and Netflix quickly became the leader in the emerging video streaming market.

Over time, Netflix has continued to disrupt its own business model, shifting more and more of its focus and resources towards streaming and original content production. The company has invested billions of dollars in creating its own exclusive TV shows and movies, such as "Stranger Things," "The Crown," and "Orange Is the New Black," which have helped to differentiate the service from competitors and attract new subscribers.

Today, Netflix is one of the most successful and influential companies in the entertainment industry, with over 200 million subscribers worldwide. The company's embrace of the "Kill Your Own Business" strategy and willingness to disrupt its own DVD rental business has been a key driver of its success and growth.

By cannibalizing its own profitable DVD business and investing heavily in streaming and original content, Netflix was able to create an entirely new market for on-demand video entertainment and establish itself as a leader in the industry. The company's success is a testament to the power of self-disruption and the importance of embracing change and innovation in the face of technological and market shifts.

The "Kill Your Own Business" strategy is a powerful approach to creating disruptive innovation from within. By proactively cannibalizing their own offerings and exploring new and innovative alternatives, organizations can stay ahead of the curve and maintain their competitive advantage in an ever-changing business landscape.

However, self-disruption is not easy. It requires a fundamental shift in mindset, a willingness to take risks, and a commitment to continuous experimentation and learning. Organizations must be prepared to challenge their own assumptions, overcome resistance to change, and make tough decisions in the pursuit of long-term success.

* * *

About the Author

Shah Mohammed is an accomplished Business Strategy and design-thinking consultant with a passion for innovation and user-centred design. He is the founder of D-Cube Designs, a leading design consultancy based in Chennai, India. With a Master's degree in Design from IIT Kanpur, India, which he obtained in 2004, Shah brings a strong academic background and a wealth of practical experience to his work.

As an Industrial Designer, Shah has played a pivotal role in successfully developing and launching over 300 products across various industries over the past decade. His expertise spans the entire product lifecycle, from conducting in-depth user research to designing intuitive and aesthetically pleasing solutions. Shah's keen understanding of customer needs and his ability to translate them into innovative product designs have earned him a reputation for excellence in the industry.

In addition to his contributions to the field of design, Shah has also established himself as a sought-after Business Strategy consultant. Leveraging his customer-centric approach, he has provided valuable insights and guidance to businesses of all sizes, helping them identify market opportunities, develop effective strategies, and drive growth. His expertise in areas such as branding, emotional branding, creativity techniques, leadership, and building competitive advantages has made him a trusted advisor to CEOs, startup founders, and aspiring entrepreneurs.

Shah is an avid blogger and has been sharing his knowledge and insights through his blog for the past eight years. With over four hundred articles covering a wide range of topics, including Branding lessons, Design Thinking, Business Strategy, and Psychology in Business, his blog has become a valuable resource for professionals seeking practical advice and inspiration.

You can connect with me on:
- https://shahmm.medium.com
- https://twitter.com/shahbaba
- https://www.linkedin.com/in/shahmm
- https://www.d-cubedesigns.com

Also by Shah Mohammed

Books on Brand Strategy, Business Strategy and Leadership

The 23 Powerful Laws of Brand Naming: How to Create Brand Names That Stand Out, Connect, and Inspire

In a world where brands are fighting for attention, crafting the perfect name can make all the difference. "The 23 Powerful Laws of Brand Naming" is your ultimate guide to creating brand names that not only stand out from the crowd but also forge deep, lasting connections with your target audience.

Branding expert Shah Mohammed takes you on a captivating journey through the art and science of brand naming, revealing the 23 essential laws that will transform your approach to naming forever.

The Timeless Laws of Branding: The Hidden Keys to Crafting Iconic Brands

Are you tired of branding books that offer fleeting trends and generic advice? Look no further than "The Timeless Laws of Branding: The Hidden Keys to Crafting Iconic Brands." This groundbreaking book unlocks the secrets to building powerful, enduring brands that stand the test of time.

The Heart Market: How to Build an Emotional Brand

In today's crowded marketplace, offering quality products or services is no longer enough. Consumers are seeking deeper connections, emotional resonance, and a sense of belonging that goes beyond mere transactions. Brands that tap into their customers' emotional core will truly thrive in the long run.

Enter "The Heart Market: How to Build an Emotional Brand" by Shah Mohammed - a groundbreaking guide that reveals the secrets to forging powerful emotional bonds between brands and their audiences. This book is a must-read for entrepreneurs, marketers, business leaders, and anyone seeking to create a brand that resonates on a profoundly human level.

The Positioning Playbook: The Winning Strategies for Market Dominance

Unlock the secrets to market supremacy with "The Positioning Playbook: The Winning Strategies for Market Dominance." This comprehensive guide dives into the art and science of strategic positioning, revealing the proven strategies that will set your business apart from the competition and propel you to the top of your industry.

Discover the power of positioning, going beyond superficial branding and slogans, to create a deep and lasting impact on your target audience. Learn how to carve out a distinct space in consumers' minds, forging emotional connections and delivering unique value that resonates with their needs and desires.

Throughout the book, readers are introduced to thirteen effective positioning strategies, each serving as a pathway to achieving market dominance and sustainable success.

Boil The Ocean: The Story of World's Amazing Brands

Embark on a captivating journey through the world of iconic brands with "Boil The Ocean: The Story of World's Amazing Brands." This thought-provoking book offers a collection of insightful case studies that delve into the successes, failures, and transformative moments of some of the most renowned brands in history.

With meticulous research and captivating storytelling, "Boil The Ocean" offers valuable insights, timeless lessons, and inspiring narratives that will engage both business enthusiasts and casual readers. Whether you are an entrepreneur, marketer, designer, brand strategist, startup owner, CEO, brand consultant, or simply intrigued by the stories behind the brands we know and love, this book will leave you inspired, informed, and eager to explore the dynamic world of branding and business.

CEO ASAP: Insider Tips from TOP CEOs for Climbing the Corporate Ladder

Welcome to the ultimate guide for aspiring leaders and young professionals aiming to ascend the corporate ladder swiftly and confidently. "CEO ASAP" is your blueprint for success, curated from the wisdom and experiences of top CEOs who have paved the way to the corner office.

Workplace Whispers: Debunking Myths and Paradoxes
Workplace Whispers: Debunking Myths and Paradoxes" is a captivating exploration of the hidden narratives that shape our professional lives. Across its pages, "Workplace Whispers" examines a diverse array of myths and paradoxes that permeate modern organizational culture. From the allure of Simon Sinek's "Starting with Why" to the pitfalls of the Growth Mindset Myth, each chapter offers a fresh perspective on familiar concepts, prompting readers to question deeply held beliefs and assumptions.

The Secret Strategies of Marketing: How Brands Use Cognitive Biases to Win Your Wallet
In a world bombarded by marketing messages, understanding the psychology that underpins consumer behaviour is the ultimate game-changer. Whether you're a marketer, entrepreneur, business owner, or an inquisitive consumer, this book unravels the mysteries behind why certain brands resonate deeply while others remain forgettable.

Your Guide to Cognitive Biases: This comprehensive guide explores a treasure trove of cognitive biases, from the well-known to the lesser-explored, offering profound insights into their applications and impact. From the allure of familiarity to the power of scarcity, you'll journey through a spectrum of biases that influence every purchase decision.

Innovation's Hidden Walls: Uncovering Limitations of Jobs To Be Done, Design Thinking, and the Diffusion of Innovation Model

In "Innovation's Hidden Walls," we delve deep into the core principles of Jobs To Be Done (JTBD), Design Thinking, and the Diffusion of Innovation Model. While these methodologies have been celebrated for sparking innovation, this book takes a critical look at their limitations. Discover how these walls can restrict your innovation endeavours, and learn how to break through them to truly transform your approach to problem-solving.

Disrupting Perfection: Uncovering the Limitations of Dieter Rams' Design Principles

"Disrupting Perfection" challenges the conventional wisdom surrounding Dieter Rams' celebrated design principles by delving into their limitations and exploring alternative perspectives on design excellence. This thought-provoking book critiques each of Rams' principles and presents compelling examples that challenge their applicability in contemporary design practice. Through insightful analysis and real-world case studies, readers are invited to reconsider established design norms and embrace a more nuanced understanding of design innovation and user experience.

SUB-BRANDING PLAYBOOK: Winning Strategies for Targeted Growth

In this captivating playbook, you'll discover a treasure trove of sub-branding strategies, each chapter unveiling a different secret weapon to unlock targeted growth. From creating sub-brands for demographic segmentation to psychographic targeting and cultural branding, we leave no stone unturned.

The book provides insights into successful sub-branding initiatives through real-world case studies, offering practical, actionable strategies for leveraging sub-brands to achieve targeted growth. By examining the considerations and criteria for developing sub-brands, readers can understand how sub-brands contribute to brand differentiation, customer targeting, and market expansion.

Elevate your brand's position, attract a loyal customer base, and surpass your competition. The Sub-Branding Playbook is your trusted companion on this exciting adventure, offering guidance, inspiration, and a roadmap to targeted growth.

Breaking Chains: A Manager's Playbook for Becoming a Leader

Embark on a transformative journey from managerial expertise to visionary leadership with "Breaking Chains: A Manager's Playbook for Becoming a Leader." This compelling book redefines leadership, offering invaluable insights and strategies for individuals striving to ascend from managerial roles to impactful leadership positions. Rooted in real-world scenarios and enriched by a wealth of leadership wisdom, this playbook provides a roadmap for professional growth and organizational success.

Unveiling the Managerial Metamorphosis: In the fast-paced landscape of contemporary business, the transition from a manager to a leader is a profound evolution. "Breaking Chains" explores this metamorphosis, unraveling the core shifts that propel individuals from functional mastery to strategic leadership. Drawing inspiration from Michael D. Watkins' HBR article, the playbook delves into transformative factors such as Specialist to Generalist, Analyst to Integrator, Tactician to Strategist, and so on.